MOONSHINE, MONSTER CATFISH, AND OTHER SOUTHERN COMFORTS

Burkhard Bilger is a staff writer for *The New Yorker*, a senior editor at *Discover*, and series editor of *The Best American Science and Nature Writing 2001*. Until 1999, he was a writer and deputy editor for *The Sciences*, where his work helped garner two National Magazine Awards and six nominations. *Noodling for Flatheads*, his first book, was a finalist for a PEN literary award for first nonfiction. He lives in Brooklyn with his wife Jennifer Nelson, their children Hans, Ruby, and Evangeline, and their coonhound Hattie.

'Fascinating... powerful... [Bilger's] lyrical narratives thrum with energy and affection. They celebrate cravings as being deeply personal, utterly illogical and irrepressibly alive.'
– *New York Times*

'If you liked *Louis Theroux's Weird Weekends*, you'll love this.'
–*Woman and Home*

'[Bilger] tenderly evokes landscape and has a philanthropic eye for the detail of other people's lives.'
–*Daily Telegraph*

'A gorgeous, humorous extended essay on a vanishing way of life in the backwoods of the American South.'
–*Esquire*

'A rare and sometimes surprising glimpse of the arcane traditions of the American backwoods and the diverse characters who keep them alive ... charming.'
–*New York Times Book Review*

Moonshine, Monster Catfish, and Other Southern Comforts

Burkhard Bilger

ARROW

For Jennifer

Published in the United Kingdom in 2002 by Arrow Books

5 7 9 10 8 6 4

First published in the United Kingdom in 2001 by William Heinemann

Arrow Books
The Random House Group Limited
20 Vauxhall Bridge Road, London SW1V 2SA

Addresses for companies within The Random House Group Limited
can be found at: www.randomhouse.co.uk/offices.htm

The Random House Group Limited Reg. No. 954009

A CIP catalougue record for this book
is available from the British Library

www.randomhouse.co.uk

ISBN 9780099415954

Penguin Random House is committed to a sustainable future for
our business, our readers and our planet. This book is made from
Forest Stewardship Council® certified paper.

Printed and bound in Great Britain by Clays Ltd, St Ives plc

Contents

Introduction

Books about strange obsessions, like the obsessions themselves, tend to grow out of chance encounters. Mine began, like an old Jack London story, with a search for a dog.

I was living in Cambridge, Massachusetts, at the time, learning to play country blues guitar and thinking it would be nice to have a lazy coonhound for an audience. In Oklahoma, where I grew up, coonhounds seem to haunt every paper route and country road, to lurk in querulous packs down every gravel drive. Most of my childhood had been spent trying to dodge their teeth, whether on foot or on my blue Schwinn bicycle. But now I found, after years on the East Coast, that I missed their voices.

That fall I started calling the AKC and the ASPCA, scanning ads in local newspapers and consulting dog trainers, all to no avail. In New England coonhounds are about as common as wolves. A few people had heard rumors of such dogs, but none had actually seen one in the flesh. Why not a pug, they said, or a nice Brittany spaniel?

Finally one day, weeks into my search, I managed to track down a breeder of blueticks. At first, as I stood on his front porch explaining what I wanted, I could see his smile fade through the screen door: his puppies were all spoken for that season, he said. But then, as we talked some more, he suddenly held up his hand. "Hold on a second," he said, turning and disappearing into his house. A moment later he emerged from the shadows with a rumpled document: *American Cooner* magazine.

It was the strangest publication I had ever seen.

—

After half a century of television, it's easy to mistake our sitcoms for ourselves—to imagine that there's no more to popular culture than Barbie dolls and TV theme songs. But *American Cooner* came from somewhere beyond the range of most antennas. Its closely typeset pages contained dozens of articles about coon hunters and their exploits, interspersed with snapshots of the hounds in action: front paws high up on tree trunks, eyes gone white from the photographer's flash, mouths bawling hysterically at a coon somewhere above. Here and there, advertisements for kennels referred cryptically to "Grand Nite Champions," "cold-nosed, chop-mouth dogs," and "chilled semen for sale." I had no idea what they meant, and it was hard to imagine that thousands of people out there did. Yet *American Cooner* was a fat, glossy monthly, chock-full of ads.

Leafing through page after page of coonhound arcana, I realized there was a side to Oklahoma that I had missed growing up, a hidden history and landscape that even locals might not see. While I had moved about in what seemed a nine-to-five world—where dinner was always at six and every porch light snapped off at ten—a few of my neighbors spent half their waking hours in the woods. When the rest of us went to bed, the coon hunters among us were just fully awakening, keyed to their dogs' unearthly voices and the forest's nocturnal pulse.

The wonder, to me, wasn't that people did such things, but that they published magazines about it and compiled coon-hunting histories, maintained century-old bloodlines, and held week-long competitions. Here was a full-blown subculture—one with its own rites, rituals, and deeply rooted lore. And I had heard of it only when I moved a thousand miles away.

In years since, I've come across even more obscure publications—a cockfighting magazine called *Feathered Warrior*, for instance—each of which speaks to a clandestine culture of its own. Few of them can be found on newsstands, just as their virtual alter egos can't be found on lists of hot Internet links. But like samizdat publications in the former Soviet Union, they reach their audience just the same.

This book explores a few of those hidden worlds— worlds that exist just around the corner, through the looking glass of American life. Each chapter circles in on a specific southern tradition: cockfighting in Louisiana, moonshining in Virginia, soul-food cooking in Georgia, and so forth. The book as a whole, how- ever, is less about the traditions themselves than the hardy, tenacious communities that have come to entangle them, like wild vines around an underground spring.

I won't pretend that the result is a comprehensive portrait, or even an internally consistent one. Reli- gion isn't here, for one thing, and race only briefly. Some of these traditions are illegal, others merely obscure; some ancient, others ultramodern. But the people who practice them share an undeniable kinship. Unlike so many of us, bent on wealth, promotion, or a few seconds of prime time, they cling to dreams that force them ever deeper underground. They hide their liquor under floorboards, make chitlins late at night when the family is asleep, or practice marbles in forest clearings. The more chilling their isolation, the brighter burning their obsessions—and their loyalty to those who share them.

I now think that rumpled copy of *American Cooner* was less a magazine than a secret handshake, the opening clue in a scavenger hunt. It eventually led me to a half-lame coon hunter in western Massachusetts and through him to a six-month-old redbone, the lonesome runt of a broken-chain litter. Hattie is a dead ringer for the dogs I grew up with (though her disposition is sweeter) and sometimes she even howls on pitch when I play the guitar. But if she helps dispel my homesickness, it's not the way I imagined. Home, she reminds me, is a place as foreign as it is familiar—one you can go back to again and again, as if for the first time.

Noodling for Flatheads

The great river was very dangerous [the Indians said]. There was a demon . . . who would engulf any who approached in the abyss where he dwelt.

—Jacques Marquette, 1673

I have seen a Mississippi catfish that was more than six feet long and weighed more than 250 pounds. And if Marquette's fish was the fellow to that one, he had a fair right to think the river's roaring demon was come.

—Mark Twain, *Life on the Mississippi*

Growing up with Lee McFarlin, I never took him for someone with odd and intimate dealings with fish. In our high school, in north-central Oklahoma, Lee was one of those kids who sort of drifted from view: cutting classes and tooling around in his '62 Chevy Impala. When I looked him up in my senior yearbook recently, he had a single picture to his name—no sports, no clubs, no academic honors. Back then, the only clue to his secret life was the faint tracery of scars along his forearms.

Late in the spring, when the rest of us were thinking about the prom, Lee would head to the Cimmaron River. As soon as the chill comes off the water, he knew, catfish look for places to spawn. Hollow banks, submerged timbers, the rusted wrecks of teenage misadventure: anything calm and shadowy will do. Once the eggs are laid, the male chases off the female with a snap of his jaws. Then for days he hovers over his glutinous brood, waiting for the first fingerlings to emerge, pouncing on any intruders.

That's when Lee would find him. Wading alongshore or diving to the lake bottom, Lee would reach into likely nooks and crevices, wiggling his fingers and waiting for a nip. When it came, he would hook his thumbs into the attacker's mouth or thrust his hand down its throat, then wait for the thrashing to stop. If he was lucky, the thing on the end of his arm was a fish.

—

Now, your average catfish is an innocuous thing: farm fed, soberly whiskered, tender as an earlobe. But inflate that fish a hundredfold—like a flea seen through a microscope—and it becomes a true American

monster. When it lunges from the river bottom, opening jaws the size of dinner plates, the suction may
pull in almost anything: shrimp, fish, snake, or rat,
baby duck or beaver. According to one old story, when
pioneer mothers did their wash by a stream, they
sometimes heard a splash and a muffled yelp: where a
little boy had been playing, only a few bubbles were
left.

It's been a long time since catfish were the stuff of
children's nightmares—the troll under the bridge, the
thing at the bottom of the well. But by all accounts
they're only getting bigger. In the 1990s more than
forty-five state records were set for catfish, including
one for a 111-pound blue cat. People spear them with
pitchforks or snag them with hooks spooled in by
lawn-mower engines; some use boron rods with titanium guides, ultrasonic lures, or baits spiked with
amino acids that seize control of a fish's brain. But a
few, like Lee, still dispense with equipment altogether.

"I'll tell you what it feels like," Lee says. "You know
little puppy dogs, when you shake the fire out of them
when they're teething? That there's exactly how it
feels." Catfish may not have fangs, but they do have
maxillary teeth: thick rows of inward-curving barbs
designed to let food in but not out. When clamped on
your arm, catfish also have an unfortunate tendency to
bear down and spin, like a sharpener on a pencil. "It
ain't nothin' but sandpaper—real coarse sandpaper,"
one hand grabber in Arkansas told me. "But once that

thing gets to flouncin', and that sandpaper gets to rubbin', it can peel your hide plumb off."

A second-generation hand grabber, or "noodler," Lee caught his first fish that way at the age of eight. Though the bite didn't break his skin, it infected him like a venom. He's married now, with two children and a plumbing business, but he still starts noodling when the wheat turns golden brown, switching to even bigger game at summer's end. His house, plain enough on the outside, is appointed in high atavistic style on the inside: heads looming from every wall, giant fish twisted in desperate poses, freezers full of strange meats. (Once, when a deer wandered through his sleepy neighborhood, Lee grabbed a hunting bow and chased it through his backyard.) Last spring, to make the place a bit more cozy, he brought home a baby bobcat.

Today, noodling with his family and me on a lake just west of our hometown, Lee needs less than five minutes to launch his boat, gun it across the lake, and leap into the water as we drift to a stop. A few seconds later he calls me over to a crumbling pier. "Sit here," he says with a weird grin, "I want you to feel something." I scoot onto the concrete, trying to look nonchalant. If Lee was enigmatic in high school, I was something worse: bookish, bilingual, taught to be terrified of the outdoors. ("The bones of drowned boys," my mother was fond of saying, "lie at the bottom of every farm pond.") While he was trapping muskrats and skinning wild pigs, I learned about the American wilderness by reading James Fenimore Cooper in German.

Sitting on the pier now, I can feel reverberations of the old panic. Beneath me, all is quiet at first. But then, as Lee fumbles under the concrete with both hands, something begins to stir. Another dip of his thick shoulders, and the thing is fully awake, thrashing in the water six inches below me, thrumming the concrete with sharp cracks of its tail. We've found it—the troll under the bridge. All that's left is to reach down its throat.

—

The origins of noodling are difficult to imagine, much less prove. In North America archaeologists have found fishhooks made of bone, weirs of wood and stone, and perforated shells for sinking nets. But noodling leaves no traces; it is as ephemeral as some of the boasts it inspires.

Native Americans, by all historical accounts, had a peculiar genius for killing fish. Hernando de Soto's men, trudging through swamps in search of El Dorado, saw lines of Indians splashing in pools, scaring up fish and whacking their heads "with blows of cudgels." Others mentioned Indians attracting fish with torches, lassoing them by the tail, harpooning them with lengths of cane, and drugging them with buckeye and devil's shoestring. The most straightforward of all fishing methods, however, was first described in 1775, by a trader-historian named James Adair:

> They pull off their red breeches, or their long slip of Stroud cloth, and wrapping it round their arm, so as to reach to the lower part of the palm of their right hand, they dive under the rock where the cat-fish lie to shelter themselves from the scorching beams of the sun, and to watch for prey: as soon as those fierce aquatic animals see that tempting bait, they immediately seize it with the greatest violence, in order to swallow it. Then is the time for the diver to improve the favourable opportunity: he accordingly opens his hand, seizes the voracious fish by his tender parts, hath a sharp struggle with it against the crevices of the rock, and at last brings it safe ashore.

Most Indians, Adair goes on to say, "are in the watery element nearly equal to amphibious animals." By contrast, the first Europeans to try their hand at noodling must have been ungainly sights. Flailing out of the water, gasping for air, they may have tried to do justice to the experience by rebaptizing it wherever they went. In Arkansas they called it "hogging," in Mississippi "grabbling," and in Nebraska "stumping," though any given noodler might have two or three names for it. In Georgia it became "cooning," in Kentucky "dogging," and in Texas and Oklahoma "noodling." "The way you get ahold of that fish," Lee explains, "it's kind of like a wet noodle, squirming and squiggling."

As settlers drifted farther down the country's waterways, catfish stories sprang up with each new town and steamboat station. According to one nineteenth-century report, catfish would congregate beneath a dam on the Kansas River "like hogs in a hog lot," just waiting to be eaten. Sometimes the same men who searched for drowning victims by the dam would strap a gaff hook on one arm and dive for fish. At the turn of the century a man named Jake Washington went down and came up two or three days later—a drowning victim himself. "He hooked him a giant fish and couldn't get loose," says Tom Burns, a self-proclaimed "old man of the river" in Lawrence, Kansas. "They found them side by side on a sandbar."

Since the great dam-building years in midcentury, American rivers have grown less hospitable to catfish. Brushy snags have been yanked clear, mucky bottoms dredged out, banks scraped clean, till the Missouri River, where some of the country's biggest blues once lurked, has become "a pretty swift ditch," in the words of one ichthyologist. If the catfish have gotten bigger lately, it's partly owing to neglect: on the Mississippi Delta, where less than 20 percent of all streams could support fisheries in 1979, the Army Corps of Engineers has nodded off just long enough for some rivers to recover.

Like the black bears resettling once-ravaged parts of the Ozarks, noodlers may be an indicator species of sorts for healthy waterways. More often than not, though, modern noodlers are less throwbacks than thrill seekers, donning scuba gear, diving into reservoirs, and harvesting fish from made-to-order catfish boxes—a southern variation on lobster traps. (One noodling pond I visited in Arkansas had such clean, accessible catfish accommodations that it was called the "hole-tel.") In Mississippi, once home to the scariest noodling waters in America, the sport's best spokesman in recent years has been Kristi Addis, Miss Teen USA 1987. One of her favorite pastimes, Addis told judges at the pageant, is grabbling for flatheads on the Yalobusha River. When pressed, she admitted that the mechanics of grabbling were "really hard to explain."

—

tick tick tick

I'm nostril-deep in murky water, sunk to the calves in gelatinous muck. Half an hour ago the troll got away, squirming through an escape hatch beneath the pier. A good omen? I'm not sure. Noodling, I know, is the fishing equivalent of a shot in the dark. For his master's thesis at Mississippi State University, a fisheries biologist named Jay Francis spent three years noodling two rivers. All told, he caught 35 fish in 1,362 tries: 1 fish for every 39 noodles. Still, it's too soon to take comfort in such statistics. From this vantage, Lee still seems dismayingly confident. Perched on the nose of his boat, surveying the shore, he looks like some raw country god, an embodiment of the lake: hair red as a clay embankment, bright puddles for eyes, patches of freckles like sandbars across broad, ruddy features. "Yessir," he shouts, "I guarantee you we're gonna find us some fish." On his best day, he adds, he caught thirty-five on this lake, all of them by hand.

tick tick tick

In the evening's honeyed light, the boulders and tumbled-down walls alongshore look ancient as Troy. "Used to be a gas station here," Lee says, wading toward a collapsed slab. "They love to hang out under this old sidewalk." Behind us, his kids have set sail from the boat in their water wings, like a small flotilla. "Daddy, can I ketch 'im, Daddy?" one of them squeals, bent on making me look bad. "You promised I could ketch one, Daddy." We shoo him away and take up positions around the rock, ready to reach in at Lee's signal.

tick tick tick

I've never been so aware of my fingers as I have been these past few days. I've found myself admiring them in pictures of myself, flexing them in the mirror, taking pleasure in their simple dexterity. Catfish, I've been told, share their love for calm, shady places with turtles, electric eels, and cottonmouth snakes. "In almost any small-town café, you can find some guy who says he knows a noodler who lost three fingers to an alligator snapping turtle," says Keith Sutton, a catfishing expert and the editor of *Arkansas Wildlife* magazine. His father-in-law, Hansel Hill, who has been noodling in rural Arkansas for forty years, had an uncle who once reached into a hole and found a "no-shoulders." The snake's bite left a permanent crook in his right forefinger. Some noodlers wear gloves; others probe holes with a piece of cane. ("If it feels rough at the end of that cane, it's a snake; if it feels like rock, it's a turtle," Hill says. "But that catfish is just as smooth and slick as can be.") Lee is a purist. Better to reach in with bare digits, he says, "so you know where you're at with that fish."

tick tick tick

"What in the hell is that ticking sound?" Lee blurts, surging from the water for breath. "It sounds like a time bomb's about to go off down there." I glance blankly at him, still focused on my wiggling fingers. "That must be my fish locator!" some local angler yells from a nearby boat. He and his buddies have been floating alongside us for a while, hoping to get in a little rubbernecking before the sun sets.

"Well, turn that damn thing off!"

Catfish have the sharpest hearing in the fish world: an air bladder tucked behind their heads serves as an eardrum, sending vibrations down an arch of tiny bones to the fish's inner ear. In Florida the Indians used to wear such bladders, dyed red, as earrings. I'm busy imagining this when I see something odd in Lee's face—a sudden tightening around the eyes. Then, just as quickly, his features relax. "You want to see him?" he says, jerking to one side involuntarily. I follow his gaze down: There, frowning beneath the water's surface, is an eight-pound flathead catfish, clearly disgruntled, gnawing futilely on Lee's thumbs. A homelier sight would be hard to imagine.

—

"Catfish are the redheaded stepchildren of America's rivers," Keith Sutton likes to say. "A lot of people think they're above catching them." My brother-in-law, George, who will fish for anything that swims, goes even further. Fish, he says, embody our social stereotypes. Haughty, neurotic, and beautiful, trout are natural aristocrats. Largemouth bass, omnipresent and resilient, are the river's working class. Catfish, in this view, are true bottom dwellers (though George says that gar, moon-eye, and paddlefish are even lower—piscine untouchables). It's an arbitrary ranking, based more on a fish's looks and personal habits than on its taste and fighting ability, but it can change the course of a river.

In the late 1980s the Army Corps of Engineers finally woke up to the untidy state of the Mississippi Delta. Twelve miles of the Yalobusha River, they announced, would be cleared, dredged, and snagged. "They said it would have no significant impact on the fish," Don Jackson remembers. "I guess they didn't think anybody would care enough to check." Jackson, then a newly appointed professor of fisheries and wildlife at Mississippi State University, decided to see for himself. Even the muddiest reaches on the

Mississippi, he found, were alive with flatheads, channel cats, carp, and smallmouth buffalo. When he told this to some of his colleagues, however, they were less than impressed. That's just fine, they said, but what about *real fish?*

Jackson and the Mississippi Wildlife Federation eventually forced the corps to scale back its plans. But most fishermen never bothered to get involved. It wasn't that they didn't care for catfish—even an ugly species can launch a thousand ships. According to the last national survey, nine million Americans catch catfish, more than fish for trout. "But the people running trotlines and hand grabbling are kind of backwoodsy," Jackson says. "They can lose things that are very important to them, and they still don't speak out." There is no environmental organization named Catfish Unlimited, no catfish-ecology chat group on the World Wide Web. Catch-and-release, an ecoreligion of sorts among fly fishermen, is practiced by only one in fifty catfish fishermen.

To born-again fly fishermen—some of whom write laws for state fish and wildlife departments—noodlers rank even lower than paddlefish. Not only do noodlers kill their fish, they grab them at their most vulnerable moments, sometimes leaving thousands of eggs behind to be eaten by predators. The fact is, however, that noodling poses little threat to the environment. A single catfish can lay enough eggs to repopulate a stream reach. Besides, noodling is just too unpleasant to become very popular. "I can't tell you how tough it was," says Jay Francis, whose 1,300 noodles had less effect on catfish stocks than did the weather. "Some of those fish were just incredibly, incredibly vicious."

If noodling is legal in only seven states, the reason has less to do with the environment than with ethics—and ethics of a perversely genteel sort. In the words of one ichthyologist in Missouri: "It's just not a sporting thing to do."

—

Stumbling across another muddy inlet, I have a hard time feeling sorry for the fish. In my right hand I'm holding a rope threaded through the gills of Lee's three catches, which swim along behind me like puppies on a leash. Blue cats have the worst bite, Lee says—"The difference between them and flatheads is like the difference between pit bulls and poodles"—but these flatheads look plenty tough to me.

A few feet from shore, the waves break across low, blue black humps, glistening beneath the water like a school of eerie, robotic fish. Two years ago Lee made these catfish dens out of sawed-up oil barrels. They were meant to be fully submerged, but the same drought that has been withering wheat crops in the Oklahoma panhandle keeps exposing these drums to the sun, forcing Lee to move them every few weeks. Wading over to one, I see that Lee has his right leg inside it, struggling to pin something against its inside wall.

"Owwwwwwwww! That damn fish bit me!"

"Have you got him?"

"Not this one, that one! The one on your line!"

I glance down at my aquatic puppies. One of them has managed to dodge through my legs, sneak up on Lee, and chomp on his big toe. A bold feat, though hardly sporting.

"Hold on a second, just hold on."

By now Lee's eyes flash signals clearly as a lighthouse: He's found a big one. In a beat I'm crouched next to him, arms tangled with his inside the den, hands splay-fingered to stop the fish's charge. Somewhere in there, a fish is caroming off the sides of the barrel, ringing it like a muffled gong. And I realize, with a shudder, that my fingers are waving frantically, almost eager for a bite.

"He's on your side," Lee yells. "Can't you feel him?"

No. But how could I miss such a huge fish? A twitch of my right hand solves the conundrum: I can't feel the fish, it seems, *because my arm is all the way down its throat.* The fish and I realize this at about the same time, like stooges backing into each other in a haunted house. The fish clamps down, I try to yank free, and the rest is a wet blur of thrashing, screaming, and grasping for gills. At some point Lee threads a rope through its mouth, and for just a second I get a good look at an enormous, prehistoric face. Then, with a jerk of its shoulders, it wrenches free, taking a few last pieces of my thumbs with it.

Later, coasting toward our dock in the dying light, Lee guesses that our catch weighs twenty-five pounds. Out of its element, though, it looks sadly diminished: prostrate on deck, mouth working to get air, skin soft and pale as dough. At first the kids scream when the boat hits a wave and the fish slides toward them, mouth agape. Then the shock wears off and their voices turn mocking, exaggerated. Finally one of them gives it a kick: just another monster done in by daylight.

But not entirely. That night, when I come home from the lake, my son comes padding down the hall to greet me. He's been hearing bedtime stories about catfish all week—stories not so different, I'll admit, from my mom's macabre tales. Now he looks up with anxious eyes as I tell him about my day. And I feel a stab of recognition, watching his face contort with the effort of imagining. The troll, I think, has found a new haunt.

Enter the Chicken

Suddenly we noticed barnyard cocks beginning
a bitter fight just in front of the door. We chose
to watch.

—St. Augustine, *De Ordine*

The road from Baton Rouge to Lafayette snakes
through the heart of Cajun country, barely elevated
above the swamp's reach. It's a dividing line of sorts
between the old Louisiana and the new, the puritan
north and the licentious south, and the land around it
seethes with fecundity. Even in the driest of seasons,
the cypress trees are moss grown and saturate, and
when the rains come the ground convulses like a living
thing. Under the highway the earth shifts and swells,
cracking the cement along its seams till it feels like a
reptile's skin beneath your car's wheels, like the back of
a great, slumbering sea beast, easily awakened.

On the night that I arrived in Baton Rouge, southern Louisiana seemed ready to cast loose from the continent once and for all. Floodwaters from the north had already strained the levees to bursting, threatening to capsize chemical barges along the Mississippi; now a thunderstorm swept in to finish the job. Driving west, beneath the phosphorescent plumes sprayed by passing cars, I felt the rain's nervous drumming in my gut. My plane had spent hours in a holding pattern above this storm, and the *kerschlick* of my tires ticked off every second of delay: midnight in the bayou seemed an inauspicious setting for a cockfight.

I was looking for a club called the Red Rooster, near a town called Maurice. A cockfighter named James Demoruelle had promised to meet me there, though I was three hours late by then and counting. Ours would be a perfectly legal meeting—cockfighting has never been outlawed in Louisiana—yet I felt as though I were going undercover. Cockfighters are strange attractors of vice, I'd been told, conduits for drugs and gambling and episodes of violence. They shun publicity like an avian virus, hide their meetings as assiduously as any drug cartel or pornography ring. A few weeks earlier I'd tracked down the editor of a cockfighting magazine at an unlisted number in rural Arkansas. When I called, she barked into the phone, "You sound like one of them animal lovers to me," and hung up.

If Demoruelle had agreed to meet me, I thought, it was because he was a little desperate. A few months before, a state congressman from New Orleans had written a bill to ban cockfighting in Louisiana. Though Demoruelle, as president of the Louisiana Gamefowl Breeder's Association, had managed to fight off "the humaniacs" for years, the battle seemed to be turning against him: cockfighting was a misdemeanor in twenty-nine states by then and a felony in sixteen. Arizona, Louisiana, Missouri, New Mexico, and Oklahoma still allowed it, but in Louisiana some of the sport's biggest boosters had been swept out of office, and in Arizona and Missouri animal rights groups were gathering signatures for state referenda on the sport.

At the same time, however, cockfighting had never been more popular. There were at least five hundred thousand cockfighters in the United States, and owing to the immigration of Asians and Latin Americans, the number seemed to grow every year. There were three national cockfighting magazines, with names like *Feathered Warrior,* and there were cockpits in even the most tranquil, law-abiding communities. When I told the name of my hometown in Oklahoma to a criminologist who specializes in cockfighting, he laughed. "Oh yeah. I know that place. There's a pit just outside of city limits."

Part of me wanted to go back and see that side of small-town life, to let it rattle my memories like the false fronts of a Hollywood set. But another part, Demoruelle must have known, was just looking for a thrill. When he wasn't fighting chickens, Demoruelle worked in a drug rehab center, and he knew all about forbidden pleasure. "Be careful," he'd told me, only half-joking. "If you get into this thing, you might really like it. I can get somebody off drugs or alcohol better than I can off of chickens."

—

Had I come to Louisiana a century earlier, the warning would have been unnecessary: cockfighting, back then, was a perfectly honorable addiction. For hundreds of years, in England, it had been a sport of schoolboys, country squires, and kings. Henry II appointed a "Hereditary Marshal of the King's Birds" to take care of his gamecocks, and Henry VIII had a sumptuous cockpit built, encircled by coops belonging to the lords and princes of the realm. Even clergymen joined in the sport, holding cockfights at churches and, in one instance, awarding a prayer book to the winner.

In the New World, cockfighting would find an even better audience. Hungry for diversion, accustomed to the brutality of frontier life, the colonists took to blood sports with indiscriminate avidity. From the Dutch they learned gander pulling and snatch the rooster: you stretched a rope between two trees, hung a bird from it upside down, greased its head with lard, and tried to yank it off as you galloped underneath.

From the British they learned everything else: bear-baiting, bullbaiting, wolfbaiting and ratbaiting, dogfighting and cat clubbing. When the first British colonists crossed the Atlantic to Jamestown, they brought fighting cocks with them.

Throughout the eighteenth century and most of the nineteenth, cockfights were a "fashionable amusement" in the North, a gentleman's pastime in the South. When cockfighting waned, in the late nineteenth century, it was out of concern less for the animals than for their audience. "By being spectators of these scenes of cruelty," one editorialist wrote, "the mind is imperceptibly hardened, and prepared for beholding, without disgust, scenes at which humanity must recoil." Others complained that blood sports sullied the national reputation or that Americans needed more fresh air, more group sports. "I am satisfied," Oliver Wendell Holmes Jr. wrote in the *Atlantic Monthly*, "that such a set of black-coated, stiff-jointed, soft-muscled, paste-complexioned youth as we can boast in our Atlantic cities never before sprang from the loins of Anglo-Saxon lineage." In 1867, New York, once famous for its cockfights, became the first city to ban all blood sports. By the turn of the century, most of the country had followed suit.

These days, Holmes would be pleased to find, American pastimes are altogether more wholesome. But then, talking to cockfighters and sociologists, politicians and animal rights activists, I often felt as though there were two Americas: the one we legislate and the one just down the street, inside an abandoned warehouse or a neighbor's basement; the one on television and the one where Santeria rituals are performed and snakes handled, where moonshine glimmers and gamecocks fight.

As I drove past Maurice city limits, the night was nearly absolute. Only now and again did the lightning expose the skeletal landscape beyond my car's headlights. I was almost to the next town by the time a low, rickety building swam into view. Turning in, I saw a few dozen pickup trucks scattered across the mud and gravel, as if flung there by the storm. Off to the side, perched on the embankment, a portable sign flickered and buzzed in the rain: "R d R ost r."

—

Demoruelle was standing on the top rung of the bleachers across the room, arms folded over his beefy chest. Though I'd only heard his voice, I picked him out of the crowd right away: silver hair, bullish features, melancholy eyes. Even at that distance he radiated a kind of sullen power, surveying the scene like Henry VIII himself, inspecting his troops.

A few weeks earlier a friend had sent me a farmer's cap with a gamecock stitched on it. Dressed in that hat, threadbare jeans, and a paint-spattered T-shirt, I thought I might slip into this scene unnoticed. But now, in the cool glare of fluorescent light, I could feel my joints stiffening and my eyes getting dodgy. I yanked off the hat and stuffed it in my back pocket.

I shouldn't have bothered. A few eyes locked onto mine as I came in, but when Demoruelle raised his hand and called me over, they drifted back to the fight. A moment later I was standing within his protective circle, shaking hands with two men who flanked him like lieutenants.

It was only then that I began to notice an odd thing: The Red Rooster was a fairly cozy place. Warm and brightly lit, high ceilinged and amiably sloppy in its construction, it seemed better suited to a Boy Scout jamboree than a cockfight. Over in the central tier of bleachers, a mother was tickling her toddler into ecstatic peals of laughter. A few rows down from her, a woman was nursing her baby within touching distance of the cocks, cupping her hands over the child's ears when their squabbling grew too loud. There were crawfish farmers in overalls and old-timers trading gossip, a woman hawking cockfighting T-shirts, and teenagers loitering in the aisles, flirting between sips of Dr Pepper. It was two in the morning by now, and the Red Rooster looked as harmless as a bingo parlor.

Where were all the drunks and scofflaws, dope fiends and edgy hustlers? Where were the "vain, idle, and wanton minds," as William Penn wrote of cock-fighters in 1682, who "gratify their own sensualities and raise the like wicked curiosity in others"? I felt like some South Sea explorer, making my way past spooky totems and grim palisades only to find a few peaceable villagers inside, eating roots and swatting at flies.

Cockfights, sociologist Clifton Bryant later told me, are like "a demographic frozen in time. The country changed, but they didn't." In 1974 and again in 1991 Bryant conducted a national survey of cockfighters. "They're mostly middle-class, from small towns or the country, more likely to be married, more likely to stay married, more likely to go to church, to be veterans," he said. "In fact, if you tried to go back and put together a typical American of the 1940s or 1950s, that would be a cockfighter."

Demoruelle's friends were typical cockers. Sonny Wabinga, to his left, was an army ranger on his third tour of duty. He had a moon-shaped face, wide, dreaming eyes, and a body as compact and lethal as any gamecock's. I'd once seen film clips of rangers on patrol so sleep deprived that they mistook tree branches for telephones and tried to call home. Surviving that sort of thing, and raising chickens, had given Sonny an oddly upbeat Darwinian outlook. "We've got the battle cross!" he told me later when I asked about his kids. "My wife's German and I'm Filipino, so my boys have the power and the speed." John Hickerson, to Demoruelle's right, was lanky and gray haired, with the loose, loquacious manner of a cowboy poet. He was from Michigan but had to come south to do his cockfighting. "Where I come from," he said, "it's a felony just to own cockfighting *equipment*."

They made a strange threesome, standing on that bench together, calling out their bets: a St. Bernard, a pit bull, and a bloodhound, all howling at the same moon. As Sonny put it, "If you have chickens, great, we can talk. Otherwise . . ." He smiled his strange smile and turned to the fight.

—

The cockpit rose from the center of the room like a miniature Thunderdome: a raised, octagonal cage, eight feet high and more than twenty feet across, surrounded on three sides by bleachers. The cage was meant to protect the audience, not to confine the birds, Demoruelle told me. "They say we're cruel, that we're making them fight. But I guarantee, if you put those chickens on either end of a football field, they'd crow and charge and end up fighting at the fifty-yard line." He spoke in a flat, faintly Gallic grumble, with flashes of local color but not much music—the voice of a man who'd never gotten used to defending himself. But I believed him. The two men entering the pit just then were cradling their birds like jars of nitroglycerin. The cocks' heads jutted from their owners' arms, wild eyed and quivering, desperate for release. From where I sat, they looked less like farm animals than birds of prey, barely a gene or two removed from gyrfalcons.

If cockfighting is still legal in Louisiana, if calling it immoral can still get your nose broken, this is why:

Most blood sports are merely cruel; no bear or badger is baited willingly, and dogs rarely fight to the death. But chickens are different. Egg factories lose as much as 80 percent of their layers to cannibalism, unless they cut off the birds' beaks; and even on a free range, roosters are seized by blood lust now and then. "We call it comin' into their pride," one chicken breeder told me. "After a storm sometimes, you'll go out into the yard and it'll be littered with dead birds."

Still, a good gamecock is largely a human invention. Beginning three thousand years ago Asian cockfighters took the most unfriendly birds on the planet—jungle fowl, *Gallus gallus*—and proceeded to make them even meaner. They crossed them with Himalayan Bankivas for speed and flying kicks, and with Malay birds for stamina and wallop. They taught them to punch and feint and roll. They marched them through gamecock calisthenics, trimmed their wattles and combs, and stuffed red pepper up their anuses. A few thousand generations later this was the result: two birds programmed to kill each other, each a glimmering alloy of instinct, training, and breeding; each as exquisitely forged and lacquered as a Persian dagger.

Below us in the pit, the two men were standing side by side now, swaying toward each other like dancers bumping hips, holding their birds at waist level and letting them peck at each other. "Gamecocks are meant to fight," Demoruelle said finally. "Anyway, they were doing it when Christ walked the earth, and he never said a word about it." Then he held up a roll of $10 bills and hollered, "Fifteen on the gray!"

Two rows down, a hairless old man with ears like flügelhorns turned and nodded.

—

Cockfighting, the *Kama Sutra* tells us, is one of sixty-four arts that every sophisticated woman should know. The rules are simple: Two roosters are matched by weight and given identical weapons (wild cocks use their bony back spurs to fight, but cockfighters cut these off and strap knives or gaffs, like curved ice picks, onto the stumps). Once armed, the birds are placed in a ring and launched at each other like self-guided missiles, exploding in a flurry of beaks and feet. The fight is no-holds-barred, but it's a controlled sort of mayhem, full of stops and starts and odd points of etiquette. When a cock stops fighting, the referee counts to twenty and then calls a twenty-second break. (In Bali they drop a pierced coconut into a pail full of water; when the coconut sinks, the birds fight.) If a cock goes down for three counts of ten and one count of twenty—or if he runs away or simply dies—the fight is over.

The whole thing can look a lot like a boxing match, but with one essential difference: Here, "gameness" matters more than landing punches. Your bird may be mortally wounded—he may even drop dead while chasing the other bird—but if he's the last one to show some fight, he wins.

Those are the basics, and any young adept could learn them in a day. But in a cockpit everything bristles with hidden meanings. Before a cock steps into the pit, for instance, the owner may lick his bird's weapons, or the referee may swab them with wet cotton and squeeze the water into the bird's beak. Both acts have a certain strange sensuality, a symbolic aptness, but the reason behind them is prosaic: Some cockfighters have a fondness for poison. On the Venezuelan island of Margarita, for example, the locals like to coat their knives with stingray venom before a fight, or they may spread a foul-smelling ointment beneath the bird's wings—when the opponent runs to escape the odor, the referee will disqualify him. Some cockfighters have been known to poison the other bird's food or else reach over and snap a small bone in his back when no one's looking.

To protect their birds, most cockfighters keep them hidden until just before a fight and sometimes put them under guard. But nothing can thwart the most determined cheater. In one famous case in the Philippines, a local mayor was at a cockpit when his bird began to lose. Rather than wait for a decision, the man pulled out a forty-five and blew the other bird away. All bets are off, he declared, since the fight never officially ended. His armed bodyguards, it seems, agreed.

—

At the Red Rooster the betting was a tad more casual—Demoruelle was the highest roller here, and he was sticking to twenties—and cheating was a rarity. Once the voices died down, the handlers set their birds behind lines of white cornmeal, eight feet apart in the dirt, and waited for the referee to shout, "Pit!" To the left was a "gray," in cockfighter's terms: a tall, lean bird with creamy hackles, gray green legs, and auburn wings. To the right was a stockier "red" with crimson hackles, yellow legs, and dark wings, his tail iridescent with ruby and turquoise. Like warrior monks, they'd both spent two days fasting, in darkness and isolation, preserving their strength and coiling their frustrations. Depending on their owners, they might be fueled by injections of testosterone, vitamin K to clot their wounds more quickly, and digitalis to speed up their already racing hearts. Now the bright lights and shouting faces were sending them into overdrive. "A bird should have a little nervousness to him right before a fight," Demoruelle said, watching them squirm, "a tremble, a twitch to him, like a boxer."

What came next, to my eyes, was an almost meaningless blur. To Demoruelle, though, it seemed to unspool in slow motion, every frame distinct: the referee's hoarse shout, unnaturally drawn out in the sudden quiet; the handlers watching his mouth, pulling back their hands as his lips pursed to speak; the cocks gathering themselves to leap, unfolding their wings as their necks strained upward; their legs driving toward each other, at the top of their arcs, talons spinning like teeth on a chain saw. And then the tumble, the scramble for footing, and another rattling clash.

"Oh. That was a good hit," Demoruelle said when the red connected with a kick to the head. "The gray's hurt." Although most hits with a gaff aren't fatal, a good cock can do plenty of damage with it. "Oh hell, yes," Hickerson said. "If you hold a plastic milk jug up to them, they can punch eight holes in it before you can pull it away."

It was all a matter of opposing forces, Demoruelle explained. "When a rooster has his wings back, he brings his feet forward and his tail down like an air brake." He raised his hands and made a few quick jabs in the air. In his twenties, he went on, he was expert at the martial arts—"135 pounds and greased-chicken-shit fast"—and I could almost see the young fighter moving beneath his middle-aged bulk. "When you're watching a cockfight," he said, "you're watching pure karate."

Both roosters were striking home now, spraying the referee with blood and bits of down. They hurled themselves at each other in weary spasms, biting each other's necks and windmilling their feet, until their gaffs snagged and the handlers rushed in to separate them. Demoruelle had hoped the gray would gradually gain the upper hand—green-legged birds have more "bottom" than yellow-legged birds, he explained—but that didn't seem to be happening. After five minutes of fighting, both birds were wounded, though the gray looked worse: one eye dim, the other destroyed, pale feathers matted with blood, beak trembling with every breath. Between rounds his handler held him close, swabbed his head with a wet sponge, and whispered to him urgently. When that didn't work, he put the bird's whole head in his mouth, sucked the blood from his throat, and then spat saliva into his beak. Little by little the gray revived, twisting his head to glare across the ring.

—

A rooster's rage is a simple thing. His courage is more complicated, and only certain weapons truly test it. So some cockfighters say, at least, and their choices divide them into camps as ardent and contrary as religious sects. In the Pacific Islands and most of North America, cockers prefer the clean, quick kill of a knife fight. (Filipinos, who like their knives especially long, sometimes forge them from armor-piercing bullets.) In India and Pakistan they breed huge, powerful Asile birds, wrap their feet to form miniature boxing gloves, and fight them for days on end. In the Caribbean and Louisiana, cockfighters tend to prefer gaffs, but even gaff fighters split into factions. Puerto Ricans cut off a bird's spur, scrape and varnish it until it's needle sharp, and strap it back on. Most Cajuns prefer their gaffs made of surgical steel, with a pointy end, but others favor a blunt gaff known as a peg awl.

Like a bullfight without a matador to finish the job,

a gaff fight can go on for hours, the cocks goring each other again and again until one surrenders from blood loss, exhaustion, or fear. On this night the gray and the red were soon lying side by side in the sand, chests heaving. But even then the gaff fight was far from over. After a moment the gray staggered to his feet and flailed about blindly, delirious with anger and pain.

"Now, that's heart," Hickerson murmured next to me. I looked over at him: shoulders hunched tight, eyes squinting slightly, a twinge of pleasure to his lips. Like most gaff fighters, Hickerson was a throwback, a believer in the ancient, primal meaning of the fight. Gaff fights are long and brutal, he admitted, but the anguish was worth it, if only for that one moment when two hearts are put to the test. "At least with the gaffs, you're really only replacing their natural spurs," he told me later. "And a gaff fight doesn't rely on a few good kicks, it relies on this." He pointed to his chest.

Over on my other side, Demoruelle started to chuckle when the red dashed away from the gray. "Did you see that guy's butt start to pucker?" he said, jerking his head toward the red's embarrassed owner. Gamecocks, for Demoruelle, were more than symbols of courage, they were stand-ins for their owners ("detachable, self-operating penises," in anthropologist Clifford Geertz's great phrase, "ambulant genitals with a life of their own"). When they collided, he didn't just see windmilling feet; he saw converging plotlines, intersecting histories: a whole community crystallized in an instant.

The gray eventually won his match and died in doing so. But the crowd barely seemed to notice. Most of them weren't here for the gambling, or the spectacle, or some terrible communion. They were here for something more mundane: a sense of community—one drawn all the tighter by secrecy and persecution. "So what do you think?" Hickerson turned and asked. I shrugged, feeling uncomfortable. "If you think it's hard for you to watch, think how it is for me," he snapped. "I've raised chickens from birth, and they're damn cute when they're little." He paused for a second, then added: "I'm a compassionate man. I have a lot of crippled roosters running around my yard that I should have gotten rid of a long time ago. It's bad business, really." Then he turned to watch the next fight, the same hungry look in his eyes.

—

Driving around Louisiana with Demoruelle and talking to him over the following months, I began to fill in the outlines of his double life. It had started, oddly enough, overseas. Although he grew up in the Mecca of American cockfighting, he discovered the sport in 1960, as a nineteen-year-old navy corpsman stationed in the Philippines. "There was this beautiful girl," he told me. "I wanted to date her, but when I finally worked my way around to asking, she said I had to meet her family first." The visit wasn't quite what he had expected. "I walked out into the courtyard and there all the men were," he remembered, "a beer in one hand, a rooster in the other."

Ever since the 1930s, when some airmen from Texas had brought their gamecocks to Manila, American birds had earned a certain mystique among Filipinos. Compared with the gaudy local strutters, the "Texas" birds were homely as could be, but they were fast and gritty, and they whipped birds up and down the island. Soon rich Filipinos were flying to Georgia or Louisiana for fresh stock, and American cockfighting magazines were worth half a bottle of Scotch. "When these guys heard that I was from New Orleans, they just went nuts," Demoruelle remembers. "They wanted to know if I knew such and such—all famous cockfighters. But this was the first time I'd ever heard of it."

He forgot about the girl eventually, but he fell in love with the birds. "Gamecocks will fight for their territory and defend it to the end," he told me. "They have a spirit about them that's very gallant." American men have very little of that spirit left in them, he says, but wherever he was stationed, he found it among cockfighters. He could stand on a hill in Borneo and listen to a rooster crow on another hill. If it was a gamecock—and he could always tell—he would knock on its owner's door, knowing he would not be refused. "I used to go out to the jungle to see fights between operations in Vietnam," he said. "I never worried about being kidnapped by the Viet

Cong, though I'm sure they were there. I was a cockfighter like them."

It was back in the States, between tours, that he had to be careful. During the day he worked at Camp Pendleton in California, but evenings and weekends he gave to gamecocks, training them in secret for airline executives and others with a taste for the transgressive. Real cockpits were hard to hide from the authorities, so he would set up in local hotels. "We used to go up the service elevators real early on Sunday morning," he remembered. "We'd fight them in a suite with a tarp thrown over the floor, a few inches of dirt on top. By noon we'd be out." Some say that cockfighting is more orderly where it's illegal, that codes of honor are more binding when they're a fighter's only guarantee. But Demoruelle disagrees. "In illegal states," he told me, "a lot of the people who do it are bad apples." Finally, in 1980, he went home to Louisiana, where he thought he had nothing to hide.

—

He lives and works back in Ville Platte now, not far from where he was born, and directs 156 employees at Evangeline Psychiatric Care. On the surface he could be a poster boy for the Louisiana tourist board: farm owner, Cajun song composer, consumer of vast racks of baby-back ribs—*"Laissez les bons temps roulez!"* Yet his double life continues. Demoruelle's posh suburban house feels barely inhabited: its oversize rooms echo beneath their cathedral ceilings, and his wife and children seem to float through them like extras on a set. "Cockfighting wives tend to be either supporters or tolerators," he says. "Mine's a tolerator—and not much of one at that."

Standing in his driveway one morning after a cockfight, I felt oddly at home. Surrounded by trim lawns and quiet neighbors, I could have been in any suburb in America. But fifteen minutes away, among rolling hills blanketed with pine, white oak, and magnolia trees, lay his game farm. And it was unlike anything I had ever seen.

When we stopped by, it was still early morning. A-frame huts, fashioned from cement or corrugated metal, marched across the weed-choked yard like miniature missile silos, their launching strips stretched out in front. Near each one a lone rooster kept vigil, often from the top of his hut, bound by one leg and screaming out challenges in ragged counterpoint to the others. "The crowing?" Demoruelle said. "That's all day. I don't even hear it anymore."

Although the farm looked like an army bivouac in miniature, these birds were more pampered than any soldier. The average broiler chicken lives for six weeks, wing to wing with tens of thousands of others. These gamecocks, by contrast, typically lived for two to three years. And they lived like pashas. Every day, from five-thirty in the morning till sundown, three employees tended to their every need. They fed, trained, and vaccinated the birds; trimmed their feathers and searched their droppings for worms; put them on trapezes to strengthen their legs and slowly stroked the twitches out of them. If the birds still went a little stir-crazy, the trainers might even bring around some nice, plump pullets to calm them down. "The prisons could learn something from us about conjugal visits," Demoruelle said. "The cocks won't fight as much if they get to see a female occasionally."

We walked around to his training room, crudely built of fiberglass and steel. An adolescent bird, or stag, begins his schooling at around nine months, Demoruelle said, when he grows his spurs and starts to show some fight. He grabbed a scruffy red bird from one of the cages lining the wall. "First we'll put sparring muffs on 'em and let 'em hit each other once or twice," he said. "Then, about six weeks before their first fight, we'll start taming 'em and workin' 'em on the bench." He walked over to a table the size of an executive's desk, padded with foam and carpet, and ran the stag through a series of drills. He shoved the stag back and forth between his hands, making him sidestep as delicately as a dancer, then pressed him down to strengthen his legs. He rolled him on his back ("that's not a natural position for a rooster") and flipped him backward through the air in a fluttering pinwheel. The bird landed deftly on his feet. "You can't train a rooster to fight," Demoruelle said. "But you're always looking for that little edge."

Every culture has its tricks for training cocks: In

Louisiana old-timers feed their birds sulfur and gunpowder. In Martinique they rub them with rum and herbs every morning. In Brittany they give them a sugar cube soaked in cognac before a fight. In Argentina, when a bird is wounded, the gauchos will rub his genitals until he ejaculates; if the sperm contains blood, the bird is retired. The one tradition that seems to cut across cultures—the one downside of training from the cock's perspective—is celibacy. Aside from the occasional conjugal visit, sex is universally believed to sap a bird of its fighting spirit, especially before a fight. In the Philippines the mere touch of a menstruating woman is said to spell doom.

Demoruelle had his share of tricks—to increase his birds' appetite, for instance, he gave them a little strychnine, which acts as a stimulant in low doses. But for the most part he put his money on exercise, nutrition, and breeding (like most American cock-fighters, he could talk genetics like a postdoc). If a stag showed promise, Demoruelle would start fighting him at around eighteen months and keep on doing it for another two or three years. Then, if the bird was very lucky and survived, he would come back to the farm to stud.

Demoruelle had a few chickens in his yard more than six years old. One of them, a dark red bird with green legs known as Crooked Toe, was nine years old and had won seven fights. "I'd love to have five hundred like him," Demoruelle said. "If I did, I'd have a

Cadillac in every garage." As it was, he barely broke even, selling birds to Hawaiian businessmen at prices ranging from $75 to $500, though a champion bird could fetch up to $25,000. "If I quit everything else, I could make a living at it—an old man's living," he said, "but I wouldn't get fat."

John Hickerson, walking next to me as we entered the feed shed, glanced around with unvarnished envy. "You have to understand that for 90 percent of cockfighters it's a losing proposition," he said. He scooped up a handful of greenish feed—a mixture of Canadian peas, corn, milo, oats, red wheat, and soy beans—from a drum the size of an oil barrel. "Look at this: nutrients. Not cheap." (Last year alone, Demoruelle's three hundred gamecocks and chicks went through some seven thousand pounds of feed.) Hickerson went over to another drum, this one filled with a pink powder. "Oyster shell and granite for their beaks and gizzards. Not cheap." Then he swept his arm in a circle, pointing to the farm, training rooms, cages, and surgery rooms. "Look around here and see the amount of work that goes into this each and every day and you'll realize that the cockfight's only the culmination," he said. "It's only the last of things."

"And you can't be a drug addict and do that," Demoruelle added. "You can't be an alcoholic."

"You have to be a workaholic."

"That's right."

When I met Hickerson, he had left behind his

family, his job, and old roots in Michigan just to live in a house next to Demoruelle's farm and raise birds. More than for any of the others, cockfighting was a way of life for him—one he had been denied up north. "We are the keepers of the chicken's genetic pool," he declared as we climbed in the van and headed for another cockpit. "We can't afford to lose this stock." Wabinga nodded quietly in the front seat. "We are the keepers of the flame."

Outside our windows, beneath a lowering sky, the swamp forest was luminous green, its trunks and branches still black from recent rain. Hickerson popped in a tape by Woody Guthrie and told me about the Calumet copper strike of 1913. When the next song came on, he stopped in midsentence and began to sing along, half smiling at the melodrama of it:

I ain't got no home, I'm just rambling 'round
Just a wand'rin' worker, I go from town to town
The police make it hard wherever I may go
And I ain't got no home in this world anymore

If ever there was a home for cockfighters, the cockpit we were visiting was it. Known as Sunrise, it was tucked along the border between Louisiana and Mississippi and drew cockfighters from the entire region. Other pits were larger: Sunset, in western Louisiana, had air-conditioning, plush seats, and a history of hosting the most famous cockfighters in the country; Texoma, on the southern Oklahoma border, had given away $150,000 at a single fight the previous year, along with a new truck for the "Cock of the Year." But as a symbol of big-time cockfighting— of what the sport might look like if it were widely accepted—Sunrise would do.

"From the sand lots of Florida to the bayous of Louisiana to the cotton rows of Mississippi and Georgia," Hickerson was saying as we passed some trailers in the parking lot, "these are some well-traveled chickens." Those at the Red Rooster, Demoruelle added, were a kind of avian underclass, poorly conditioned and sloppy in their attacks. These birds were in a different league. Each owner had paid $300 for the right to enter six of them in the derby. Because 150 owners were signed up in all, that came to nine hundred chickens fighting for one $45,000 pot. "That guy over there?" Demoruelle said, pointing to a middle-aged man in jeans and a sport shirt. "He's the largest fish wholesaler in Mississippi."

The whole scene reminded me of Samuel Pepys's description of a cockfight in seventeenth-century London: "But Lord! to see the strange variety of people, from Parliament . . . to the poorest 'prentices, bakers, brewers, butchers, dairymen, and what not; and all these fellows one with another cursing and betting." And yet I kept coming back to those nine hundred chickens. A cockfight, as I understood it, was a single combat between lone fighters. But this sounded more like a mass slaughter, a battle royal. True, not all nine hundred birds would fight: a cockfighter would stay in the contest only so long as his birds were undefeated. (In Martinique the list of matched roosters is called a *tableau de mariage*.) Still, a good half of the birds would enter the pit tonight, and half of them might die.

Sunrise, at first glance, hardly seemed the place for such epic carnage. Slapped together of corrugated steel, painted sky blue, and thrust into a patch of scrub oak, it had an almost deliberate impermanence about it, as if it could be disassembled with a moment's warning and spirited into the woods. As we shouldered our way through the front door, one of the men we passed shook his head and said, "It's a madhouse in there. You can't even get a seat." But we pushed ahead anyway, past concession stands, surgery rooms, and bloody drag pits where the endgames of the longest fights were played out, past walls of raw particleboard and through leaning, unsquare spaces. Though we never descended any stairs, we seemed to be tunneling underground, the heat pipes like earthworms glistening in the walls. When a long corridor opened at last onto the cockpit, it felt like an animal's burrow, spacious yet claustrophobic.

The bleachers rose in a steep-sided bowl around us, two stories high and bristling with spectators. This was no neighborhood social club, like the Red

Rooster. These people had paid $16 a seat and traveled hundreds of miles to be here, and they focused on the pit below with clenched jaws. There was a sense of volatility in the air, of minds at the edge of ignition, and I kept imagining the chaos if a grease fire erupted in the concession stand and we had to claw our way back through those tunnels.

The pit itself, by contrast, was a model of neatness and grim good order. Most of the birds wore one-inch Spanish knives or three-inch Filipino knives on their heels, and their bouts were often over within seconds. A Filipino knife, driven by a powerful gamecock, can split a bird's head in a single stroke, and Spanish knives are nearly as deadly. ("I know a thoracic surgeon who handles his own chickens in the ring," Hickerson had said on the ride over. "Now, how can you be that smart and that dumb at the same time?") The referee would cry, "Handle!," the birds would flurry in the air a few times, and then one or both of them would lie dead. No bludgeoning brawl, no show of courage or fear, surprisingly little blood.

Should cockfighting ever make it onto *ABC's Wide World of Sports,* I thought, this was how it would be: a little trash talking between the handlers, a little fancy footwork by the birds, and then the knockout blow. Watching a gaff fight required a nearly religious devotion, a hard slog toward an uneasy enlightenment. But a knife fight offered instant gratification. It was all highlight film and no story. Throw in a few bets, to give yourself a stake in the outcome, and you had the ultimate in guilty pleasures.

Now I could see why Demoruelle had thought cockfighting might seduce me. If he preferred knives to gaffs, it was partly because the fights were shorter and they gave him more chances to gamble. But part of him, too, had come here to see something killed. "Man is born a warrior," he told me later, "and the more we constrict his natural tendency to hunt and to kill, the crazier the world seems to become." After ten or fifteen bouts, though, Hickerson began to fidget. "Knives are going to kill this sport," he muttered. These cocks weren't bred for courage, they were bred for speed and power. Knife fights were mostly about luck and getting in the first punch, Hickerson said. Knife fights were a crapshoot.

As for the crowd, a crapshoot was exactly what it wanted. Whenever a gaff fight began, people's attention went slack, and they drifted into small talk. But as soon as two knife fighters came out, they seemed to hold their breath. Soon the bets began to ring out, shyly at first, then with more urgency as some failed to find takers: "Ten on the red!" "I'll take twenty on the white shirt's bird!" A few rows over, a man handed some bills to his skinny boy and whispered instructions in his ear. The boy jumped on his seat, screwed up his face, and screamed an octave above the rest of the crowd: "Twenty on the red! Twenty on the red!"

This was where things got interesting at many Asian cockpits. Small-time fights were merely about money, but bigger ones were about status and kinship—you always bet on your kin group's cock, and you did so for prestige, not winnings. But the bets at Sunrise, unlike those at the Red Rooster, were as impersonal as coins tossed into a slot machine—six roosters in a row and you hit a jackpot. Hickerson, for his part, hardly bothered to assess the birds. When knife fighters came into the pit, he almost always stood up and yelled, "Twenty-five–twenty! Twenty-five–twenty!" meaning, "You choose the bird, but I get twenty-five dollars if mine wins, and you get twenty if yours wins." As long as a cockfight is just a game of chance, he said, you might as well play the odds.

The fights would go on like this till dawn—there were a lot of chickens to get through. At one point I stepped into the bathroom and found a referee scrubbing the blood from his face while a line formed behind him. He kept squinting into the mirror, face sopping wet, and then bending down to scrub some more. Finally he glanced at my reflection and laughed.

"Stuff still isn't comin' off!"

"Must get pretty thick by the end of the night."

"Heck, yeah, I'll be covered in it head to foot. These white stripes won't be white no more."

The owners were honor bound to stay till the end, but we were only spectators, so we slipped out before midnight. By then there were dead cocks lying in the hallways and heaped in trash barrels, their bodies twisted and brittle, their once-brilliant feathers dimmed by dried blood. "We used to eat the losers after a fight," Demoruelle said in passing, "but the dewormer some people use now makes the meat carcinogenic."

Surreal as it was, the scene made a certain sense. At pits like Sunrise, cockfighting was big business—less folk tradition than mass-market entertainment—and the audiences were hardly different from those at riverboat casinos in Baton Rouge. The cocks we had seen, impeccably trained though they were, had lost much of their glamour to commerce. Elsewhere they might be symbols of sin or sexuality, courage or betrayal, stand-ins for their owners or for the devil himself. But at Sunrise a gamecock was just another form of disposable culture.

—

In Bali, Clifford Geertz once wrote, a cockfight is a story that people tell themselves about themselves. For more than two centuries the same was true in this country. Long before the Revolution, George Washington loved a cockfight for the spirit of anarchy that it embodied, and he once invited Thomas Jefferson to Mount Vernon to see his "yellow pile" gamecocks. By the 1830s Andrew Jackson was fighting cocks on the White House carpet, and cockfighting was a national pastime—an embodiment of the country's new arrogance. Three decades after that, Abraham Lincoln, a former cockfighting referee, saw something darker and more ambivalent in it: "As long as the Almighty permits intelligent men, created in His image and likeness, to fight in public and kill each other while the world looks on approvingly," he is reported to have said, "it is not for me to deprive the chicken of the same privilege."

But nowadays blood sports are a story we would rather forget. In the fall of 1998 volunteers with anticockfighting groups in Missouri and Arizona managed to gather 136,000 and 189,000 signatures, respectively, forcing state referenda on the sport. In early polls, 88 percent of Missourians said they were against cockfighting, and 87 percent of Arizonians, but in the privacy of the voting booth, many must have had second thoughts: only 63 percent voted against the sport in Missouri and 68 percent in Arizona. Still, today, hosting a cockfight is illegal in both states, and as I write, Oklahomans are petitioning for a referendum of their own.

Only in Louisiana, where the sport once seemed most vulnerable, do cockfighters feel a measure of security. Twenty years ago, when Louisiana passed a new set of animal rights laws, cockfighters had to dabble in taxonomy to avoid them: chickens are not animals, they declared in an amendment pushed through at the eleventh hour; they are birds. Since then, cockfighting has never been seriously threatened: the anticockfighting bill that Demoruelle feared never even made it past committee. The next year, when an anticockfighting amendment reached the floor of the house, it was defeated by a vote of 22 to 5.

Nevertheless, most observers say that legal cock-fighting will be gone within the next ten years. Even in Louisiana, a single election and a new crop of legis-lators could consign cockfighting to the chopping block. "I think the forces of modernity and New South boosterism are just going to do it in," says Frederick Hawley, a criminologist at Western Carolina Univer-sity who wrote his Ph.D. thesis on cockfighting. "And if I'm wrong now, it won't be long before I'm right."

—

Animal activists will tell you this fight is all about morality. Cockfighters will tell you it's about individual liberty. Most legislators, if you catch them in an honest moment, will tell you it's about economics—about the South reinventing itself to attract investors. But mostly it's a matter of demographics: the more urban an area is, the more likely it is to ban the sport. And though country values have given way to city values, cockpits to Kentucky Fried Chicken, the sum total of bloodshed has hardly been diminished, only swept out of sight.

Not long after I left Louisiana, I went to visit a chicken factory an hour south of Little Rock, Arkansas. One of forty-one "vertically integrated" operations owned by Tyson Foods, this one took in 1.3 million birds a week and spat out an endless stream of chicken parts and precooked wings. A mill, a hatchery, and dozens of feed sheds lay around it like spokes on a wheel, and most of the work was automated (when a chicken laid an egg, a tiny conveyor belt beneath the roost trundled the egg off for incubation). Thanks to such efficiencies, American factories slaughter some seven billion chickens a year, and chicken meat, once more expensive than filet mignon, has become blandly ubiquitous—poor man's fare. Breeders, meanwhile, keep picking up the pace: a century ago a broiler needed sixteen weeks to reach two pounds; today they reach four pounds in six weeks.

My guide at the factory, a man named Archie Schaffer III, was a rare believer in full disclosure (the public relations people at Perdue wouldn't let me near their factory). "Nobody has any idea in America where their food comes from," he told me, "and the reason is people like me." Schaffer was more than happy to show me the hatchery, where eighty-five thousand chicks tumble down chutes every hour, like cotton balls at a cotton ball factory; the vast hangars where the chicks grow into broilers; the trucks that haul the broilers to the factory seven thousand at a time. Yet when I asked to see the killing floor, he nearly refused.

I could see why. If a broiler's life sometimes looked like a trip to the amusement park—careening up and down conveyor belts, standing in crowds, watching gizmos pop and whir—this was the nightmarish finale, the tunnel of fear. After their wild ride in the truck, the birds were dropped onto a broad belt that rolled into the dark mouth of the factory. Inside, most of the room was bathed in black light—it calms the birds down, I was told—and the stench of spilled intestines was overwhelming. Assaulted by screaming machinery and Top 40 radio, the birds were jerked from the belt by a row of eight workers, wearing black goggles and industrial tunics, and hung by their feet from a running chain overhead. "The live hang job is about the nastiest job in the business," Schaffer shouted. "But a lot of people seem to like it."

Next door was a room of raw concrete, lit like an old Dutch painting, with a bright, bloody trough snaking along the wall. "First we stun 'em over here," Schaffer explained, pointing to the first of two mechanical bottlenecks through which the chickens' heads had to pass. "Then we slice 'em with a rotary saw over there." Most of the birds stretched their necks obediently. But every so often one would crane his head to see where he was going—and inadvertently avoid the saw. When that happened, a nearby attendant, sitting on a stool, would reach over and slit the rubbernecker's throat.

These are things we don't want to know, that we zone away beyond city limits, and most meat producers are happy to oblige us. Every year we eat more chicken meat and see less and less of the living birds, and this strikes us as right and normal. Animal rights activists, of course, condemn poultry factories as well as cock-fighting, but most of us aren't that consistent. We're appalled at blood sports, yet when activists picket slaughterhouses or send lurid photos to the media, we resent them, deem them unrealistic. Like cockfighters, they threaten a cherished illusion: that society, in growing up, has lost its taste for blood.

——

When I was nine years old, and the only blood sports I knew were those my brother had invented, my family rented a house with some chickens in the backyard. It was a crumbling old adobe in a quiet part of Pasadena, where my father would do research in the summer, and the chickens seemed to have been there forever. After a while I got used to their sudden flights of rage when I fed them, their strange, hysterical secrets. But I never got used to the dawn. In suburbia, more than most places, a cock's crow can sound like the end of the world.

One afternoon, when my mother answered a knock on the door, she found a policeman standing awkwardly on our stoop. "It's about your rooster, ma'am," he said.

My mother stared at him blankly for a moment. Then, with a twitch of a smile, she asked: "What's he done?"

Our bird was arrested for disturbing the peace. After

the Humane Society dragged him away—kicking and screaming as only a chicken can—we never saw him again. Looking back, we always laughed at my mom's reply and at the rooster in the paddy wagon. But the funniest part, we thought, was the fact that we had a suburban chicken coop in the first place. Now I think that the joke was on us. We thought of our neighborhood as an ideal of sorts, clean and safe and free of life's old brutality. But we lived in a glass bubble, one so fragile a rooster's call could shatter it.

These days the stories we tell ourselves about ourselves grow ever more polished and predictable. We play out our primal urges on the Internet, in cineplexes, or in therapy rather than in the town square at midday. Yet cockfighters still stir in the dark, incubated by secrecy and the heat of resentment. Judging from the pits I visited, the twilight suits them best. "You can't stop us," Demoruelle says. "We have more gamecocks being fought this year than we've had in the history of this country." If they jangle a few nerves, so be it: disturbing the peace is a rooster's business.

Moonshine Sonata

Smith Mountain Lake lies in the foothills of the Blue Ridge Mountains of eastern Virginia, an hour's winding, tumbling drive from convenience store or neon sign, fast-food joint or freeway. On still summer days millworkers and tobacco farmers from Roanoke and Danville like to go there with their ice chests and portable TVs, pitch their tents among the dogwood and magnolia, and imagine what it might have been like to carve a living from country so rough, to raise a family and erect a cabin and hunt for food among the parsimonious trees. At the lake's visitor center, perched on its shores, they can see sepia photographs of their ancestors and a few examples of the tools they used, now weathered and gray. There is a wooden scythe and a handmade lathe, a corn cutter, a rusted sausage stuffer, and a wooden trap for catching small mammals. And over in the corner, seemingly more ancient and obsolete than all the rest, stands a small still used for making moonshine.

Press a button on the oak barrel, cup the old-fashioned ear horn to your head, and you'll hear a running stream and a lazy banjo, footsteps splashing stealthily through a swamp, and waterbirds squawking at their approach. A voice will tell you that the dictionary defines moonshine as illegally distilled whiskey and that it earned that name because it was often made under cover of night. You'll learn that moonshine is made from a mash of grain, yeast, sugar, and water, that this mash is fermented and boiled, and that the alcoholic fumes are cooled to liquid in a long, twisted copper pipe known as a worm. You'll learn that making moonshine is an ancient, exacting craft, but it was outlawed in 1791, when the federal government under George Washington imposed a tax on all liquor.

Most of what you'll hear is common knowledge, long ago passed into folk tales and history books. But if you had come to that same place one winter morning in 1993, equipped with a high-powered telescope, you might have gotten a more up-to-date education. Training your scope across the lake's clear waters, toward a steep hill that looms beyond the southeastern shore, you would have made out seven figures huddled in the snow, barely discernible in their camouflage parkas, patiently watching a long silver shed below them.

Just a few days before, on Christmas Eve morning, J. E. Calhoun, then a special agent with the county sheriff's department, had gotten a call from a local farmer. "It sure smells sweet down here," the man had said. "I ain't never been around no liquor still before, but if I had, I'd swear it would smell like that." When Calhoun came around later that day, he caught the scent right away: a heady, yeasty presence in the air, as if every cook in the neighborhood had decided to bake bread at the same time. The smell had a hint of malt to it, like a strong beer, and just a trace of bitterness—of something slightly rotten at its core. Somewhere close by, it told him, some mash had just finished fermenting and bootleggers were running their still.

For the next two weeks Calhoun spent nearly every night on that hillside, sipping coffee and soup from thermoses and scanning the valley with binoculars. Because bootlegging is a tax violation rather than a criminal offense, he was joined by four revenue agents with the Virginia Alcohol Beverage Control Board as well as a local sheriff. "The still was runnin' that first afternoon," Calhoun says. "But before we could make a move on it, they was shuttin' down." When the search warrant was finally ready, and the agents came rushing down the hillside with their walkie-talkies and guns at the ready, the moonshiners had taken off. Yet what Calhoun found left him dumbfounded.

Inside the forty-five-by-ninety-foot warehouse were thirty-six 800-gallon pots, each nearly filled to the brim with fermenting mash. There was so much mash that the smell had carried through six inches of insulation and tar paper; so much mash that Calhoun and the others were afraid that dumping it might disturb the pH balance of the lake. (In the end, they pumped it out and shipped it to a water-treatment plant.) Four submersible pumps ran water to the still from a nearby pond, stacks of sugar and yeast fifteen feet high kept the fermenting mash well fed, and bales of shrink-wrapped gallon milk jugs stood ready for transport. Altogether, the setup was capable of producing some four thousand gallons of whiskey every seven days—more than enough to keep a small city inebriated.

The Smith Mountain bust was the single largest in Virginia history, yet its details feel somehow anachronistic, like the herky-jerky footage from an old new reel. In weeks of traveling through the South researching moonshine, I was told again and again that moonshining is a dying art, too demanding and unprofitable for modern criminal tastes. Federal statistics bore this out: In 1970 the Bureau of Alcohol, Tobacco, and Firearms seized 5,228 stills and 86,416 gallons of liquor; by 1996 those numbers had dropped to a single still, and it was bone dry. "It used to be our forte, sitting on stills," a publicity officer for the bureau told me, "but by the time I got here it was long gone." The note of nostalgia in his voice was unmistakable.

When I talked to local revenue agents, though, I got a very different story. There may be more moonshine in circulation today than thirty years ago, they said; the feds simply ignore it in favor of the war on drugs and terrorists. Gone are the Eliot Nesses, busting up stills with religious zeal; in their place are working-class detectives on tight budgets, squeezing in a few moonshine raids now and then between shipments of cocaine. Even so, between 1985 and 1998 agents in six Virginia counties alone seized 538 stills. "People keep saying that the moonshiners have gone, but we keep finding more stills," one agent told me. "I guess if no one prosecuted murderers, they wouldn't exist, either—there'd just be a bunch of dead people lying around."

—

It was neither a revenue agent nor a publicity officer who took me to see the site of the Smith Mountain still, but a local moonshiner I'll call Jim Stoat. We drove there on a dreary October morning, when the leaves of the surrounding forest were as faded and lifeless as spent mash, but to Jim the place still held a glamorous glow. Parked at the foot of the mountain, we looked up at the slope where the agents had done their stakeout. A tall wrought-iron gate, surmounted by gilded eagles, fronted the property, a white gazebo stood in the middle distance, and the silver shed glimmered beyond it. Everything about the place was contrary to the old moonshiner's creed, which preaches mobility over permanence, humility over ostentation, yet Jim couldn't help but admire its scale, its chutzpah. The shed was snugly built, there was enough water to supply a hundred distilleries, and the owner bought his grain from a hog farmer who lived down the road. "Thirty-six pots," Jim said, pausing to do the math in his head. "That's fifteen thousand pounds of sugar alone." Standing there gazing at the golden eagles, he looked like a small boy at the gates of Xanadu, dreaming of his own mansion on a hill.

In most ways Jim ran his business like any other young entrepreneur. He kept track of the moonshine market and adjusted his prices accordingly, monitored product quality and looked for ways to streamline production. While others scanned the *Wall Street Journal,* he kept a file of clippings from local papers, noting which colleagues had been busted, what kinds of sentences they were given, the size of their stills, and where they were established. He knew which cars the local agents drove and kept track of their movements whenever he was running a still.

The differences were largely a matter of style and degree of risk. Instead of three-piece suits, Jim favored T-shirts and baseball caps; instead of lawyers, he tended to back up his deals with firearms. Rolling around on the floor of his car were two boxes of hollow-point .357 cartridges for his snub-nosed Smith & Wesson revolver, along with copies of *Guns and Ammo* and *Shooting* magazine. Propped next to his seat, like a second gearshift, was the tarnished bronze handle of a long, medieval-looking dagger. "They call this an Arkansas toothpick," he told me as we drove. It was meant for whacking, not stabbing, he added reassuringly, but I knew that this part of Virginia had had its share of moonshine-related killings. "They have got to be the most paranoid people in the world," one agent told me. "They're always thinking that somebody told on them, and that fuels the cycle of violence." Only a few months earlier, two bootleggers from the same family had shot a third to death; two years before that, Jim's own mentor had been gunned down in his car.

These facts made me nervous, but not nearly as nervous as I made Jim. Under other circumstances, I think, we might have taken an instinctive liking to each other. We were both in our early thirties and both had three-year-old boys. Jim liked to talk, I liked to listen, and we both had a love for the detailed inner workings of a craft and a business like moonshine. Still, the fact was that he was a felon, in a business rife with undercover agents. And though I had no intention of giving him away, I was dividing my time between him and the revenue agents bent on hunting him down. He was savvy enough to suspect as much—he'd even given me the local sheriff's name, in case I wanted to interview him—but the situation made him justifiably uneasy. "Never sell to someone you don't know," was the first rule of moonshining. Or as Jim's father, a moonshiner himself, put it: "Dealin' with strangers is like bitin' a persimmon. If the fruit ain't ripe, it'll turn your mouth inside out."

—

I first met Jim at a "moonshiners' reunion" in northwestern South Carolina, in an area known as Dark Corners. We had both heard of the event through the Internet, while doing random searches for the keyword "moonshine," and had both come with a certain skepticism. The organizer, a grizzled hippie musician named Barney Barnwell, claimed to descend from a long line of moonshiners, and he promised that plenty of ex-moonshiners would be in attendance. But at first glance the moonshining theme seemed largely a marketing ploy. There were crafts booths and barbecue stands, bluegrass concerts and tours of defunct stills. Though Dark Corners, with its dense forests and secret glens, was once a notorious haven for bootleggers, these days most people made their living from the BMW plant in Greenville.

At night, when the last band left the stage, we'd retire to campfires in the woods, among the creepers and crickets and trees hung with Confederate flags. The guitars and mandolins would chime on till morning, and people would pass around the old stories—of stills hidden behind false walls and under cemeteries, of car chases through the ivy-hung Carolina hills, of judges going home from court half-drunk on "corn squeezin's." But the heroes were invariably neighbors, or relatives, or men long dead, and there was more marijuana smoke in the air than illegal spirits. When I asked one supposed bootlegger for a taste of his wares, he gave me a half gallon of pickled peaches instead.

Only late in the reunion did I get stronger proof of a living tradition. Up on stage, Barnwell's heavy-metal bluegrass group, The Plum Hollow Band, was finishing its last set. "I used to hate my daddy's music," he said before launching into a medley of "Rocky Top" and a Black Sabbath song, "but now I think we have some common ground." When it was over, and the crowd was whooping and laughing and lifting its lighters in mock tribute, he went back to the mike and announced an impromptu "'shine-tasting" contest. "It's illegal as hell," he said. "But what are they gonna do, arrest five hundred of us?"

It was as if some silent code had been broken. Within a matter of minutes mason jars were making their way through the crowd from every corner: some filled with moonshine clear as water, others afloat with strawberries, blackberries, scuppernong grapes, and native peaches. Barnwell entered a little white lightning, a little peach, and a little wild muscadine. Another contestant walked past me balancing half-gallon jars on each shoulder. "I've got to mail these to

California tomorrow," he said, "but I might as well have a taste first."

Word had gotten around, over the previous few days, that a clan of bootleggers had come down from Franklin County, Virginia, and that moonshine was still serious business up there. To guard against charges of nepotism, and to give the contest a somewhat cosmopolitan flavor, Barney chose the patriarch of their clan, Jim's father, Willard, as the judge. (I've changed the names of Jim's family members, as well as some identifying details about them.) Willard was a short, wizened septuagenarian, with gnarled hands and lidless, protruding eyes. As he lifted each entry from a row of numbered Dixie cups, his eyebrows would arch and his eyes would go wide. "Ah-ooooh," he'd say, smacking his lips. In the end he declared Barnwell's white lightning the best straight moonshine and Barnwell's cousin's peach the best of the fruits.

Afterward, I cornered the old judge, hoping that the tasting might have loosened his tongue. At first I found him more than accommodating. He told me how to make peach brandy and how to test moonshine for quality: "Strike a match to it and look at the flame: if it's blue, it's all right, but if it's yellow . . ." He told me that homemade liquor has fewer chemicals than store-bought, that the body naturally manufactures a quart of alcohol every day, and that moonshine could help you pass a kidney stone. But when I asked him about his own stills, he drew back into his shell like a snapping turtle. "I never have made any liquor," he said, glaring at me from beneath the shadow of his cap. "My mama used to give it to me for the whoopin' cough, with a spoonful of sugar, but that's about all."

I might have given up then, if Jim hadn't suddenly appeared, bobbing his son on his knee. He'd come to Dark Corners to check out the competition, he said, and he wasn't too impressed. The few active moonshiners around were mostly home brewers, and after days of their tall tales and empty boasts, Jim positively fidgeted with the need to set the record straight. Every time the old man tried to duck a question, Jim would jump in with the answer: market prices, manufacturing methods, preferred means of camouflage. "This ain't nothin'," he said, glancing at the two rusted stills on display beside us. "This ain't nothin'."

In the background I could hear four singers patiently build their harmonies, while a fiddle and banjo tripped madly along behind:

Now pour a glass of 'shine to fortify your soul.
We'll talk about the world
and the friends we used to know.
Well, I see a stream of girls
who'll put me on the floor.
The game is nearly over, the hounds are at my door.

Franklin County, Virginia, unlike most places renowned for their moonshine, seems at first glance to have nothing to hide. Compared to the huddled hills of Dark Corners, the landscape here is open armed and welcoming, lush with tobacco and spreading oaks and braided by slow-moving streams. In autumn the county roads burrow through the forests like children in a leaf pile, leaping up into sunlight on the other side; the mountains hover above the horizon in pale blue outline, and curing barns keep watch from every hillside, their timbers warped and cracked and mortared with red earth. It's a landscape as lovely as it is innocuous—one that's easy to hurtle past as you head toward some more dramatic vista—and the locals like it that way.

The town of Zenith, where Jim lives with his wife, Kelly, and his boy, Audie, is hardly less humble, its name notwithstanding. Whether it's really a town or just a minimart at a fork in the road is a matter of some local debate. Maps don't show it, phone operators don't list it, and letters come addressed to a larger town, twenty-five miles to the west. The surrounding area is so sparsely inhabited, and so many turns from a well-traveled highway, that people invariably wave to every passing car—not just to be friendly, but because they assume that they know the driver.

Jim's double-wide mobile home sits about five miles from the minimart, a stone's throw from a Presbyterian church. Unlike his neighbors' houses, it's placed far back from the road, screened from view by a row of white pines and guarded by a myopic, mean-spirited dog named Goober. From his front window you can see his father's house—a yellow, three-story structure slightly a-kilter from when it was moved from beside the church—and through his back window you can see the remains of the log cabin where his mother was raised. For at least six generations, he says, his father's people have lived within thirty miles of this place, marrying next-door neighbors or cousins as often as not. And though, for a time, Jim wanted nothing more than to get away from Zenith, he eventually married the girl next door as well.

Jim's people have been making liquor since as far back as Willard's limited recall will allow, and the outline of their history is roughly that of all moonshining in America. There were three Scotch-Irish brothers, family legend has it, who came first to Pennsylvania and then moved south to Virginia, making whiskey as they went. Just when they arrived is unclear, but they most likely belonged to the great wave of Scotch-Irish settlers that flowed down the Great Philadelphia Wagon Road between the 1730s and the 1770s. Known as Ulstermen, after the part of Northern Ireland from which they hailed, they had come to America fleeing smallpox, sheep rot, drought, and winter fevers, but especially repressive land policies. Tireless farmers, they had introduced the potato to Ireland and turned miles of bog into productive farms, only to have their rents doubled or tripled when the leases ran out. Great lovers of "ardent spirits," they had refined the arts of Scottish and Irish whiskey making, only to have a crushing excise tax placed upon their wares. Once in America, they were hungry for their own land and positively allergic to government. They gravitated toward the wildest, roughest sections of land, tamed them as they had the Irish bogs, and kept their own counsel. When Pennsylvania grew more crowded and less welcoming, they headed south across the Susquehanna River, along the Alleghenies, and down the Shenandoah Valley, dropping off Jim's ancestors along the way, presumably, before moving on to the Carolinas.

American history, some say, could be written in terms of whiskey as well as wars and wandering tribes, and the result might say more about the American character—about the perennial battle between liberty and the rule of law. Since the beginning, liquor making was an essential frontier enterprise, whether in the Caribbean, where rum fueled the economy, or in the early colonies, where newcomers were advised to distill liquor until their stomachs got used to the water. To a farmer, a still was the ideal instrument for concentrating profits: a horse could carry only four bushels of corn at a time, but it could carry twenty-four bushels in liquid form. And to every colonist alcohol was far more than a means of getting drunk. It was a disinfectant, a tranquilizer, and a medicine for countless ills. It was an anesthetic, a solvent, and an admirably stable unit of currency.

No wonder, then, that the liquor tax of 1791 provoked the first armed revolt in the young country's history. (Alexander Hamilton, the architect of the tax, seems to have intended just such a reaction, if only to give the government a chance to prove its mettle.) Though the Whiskey Rebellion was soon lost, the same battle would be fought again and again on a lesser scale. Thomas Jefferson repealed the tax in 1802, bringing on a brief golden age for small distilleries, but Abraham Lincoln reimposed it in 1862 to raise money for the Civil War. That act also created the Internal Revenue Service, with whom moonshiners have been at war ever since.

In his 1974 book, *Mountain Spirits,* writer Joseph Dabney pegged Dark Corners, Dawson County, Georgia; Cocke County, Tennessee; and Wilkes County, North Carolina, as the historic moonshine centers. But in the past twenty-five years that geography has shifted. While some areas have stepped up production, others have switched to more profitable poisons. When Barnwell went to jail in South Carolina in the 1970s, it wasn't for making moonshine, like his grandfather, but for growing marijuana. (After that, he grew hallucinogenic mushrooms in the same mason jars his grandfather used for moonshine.) When I interviewed the grandson of Dawson County's most famous bootlegger, he was in county jail for possessing methamphetamine with intent to sell.

"I kind of went from moonshine to marijuana to

crank," he explained one morning, sitting across from me at the police station, wearing bright orange coveralls from his work-release program. "When I was a kid, I used to tote sugar for my grandpa's still. Then I ran the ground crew for my dad, when he'd fly in his crop from Honduras—two-hundred-pound bales of marijuana comin' out of the sky, right here in the foothills of Dawsonville." Methamphetamine, or crank, was now the drug of choice in Dawson County, he said, and so many people were making it that the quality was getting dicey. "I guess you could say liquor was the root of everything."

Franklin County may be the last of the old watering holes that hasn't gone dry. During the 1930s nine out of ten people in the county had some connection to illicit alcohol, a federal commission reported, and author Sherwood Anderson based a short story on a famous moonshine conspiracy there. Now local moonshiners have taken the lessons of that era to heart, preselling their liquor to networks of shot houses, mass-producing it, and keeping the quality just high enough that it won't kill people. Though the landscape may not lend itself to secreting stills and running from revenuers, major moonshine markets encircle it like spigots on a keg: Philadelphia to the north; Washington and Richmond to the east; Raleigh, Greensboro, and Charlotte to the south; Charleston to the west—most of them less than three hours away. Moonshiners in Virginia produce close to a million gallons a year, the lion's share of it in Franklin County. Yet according to the Virginia Alcohol Beverage Control Board, 60 percent of local moonshine is sold out of state, mostly to inner-city blacks, and almost none of it is sold within the county. Homemade liquor, these days, is meant mostly for strangers.

—

Jim rubs his eyes and goes over the numbers one more time, whispering so as not to wake Kelly and Audie in the next room. The early morning light, filtering through the room's dark blue curtains, gives the air a spectral glow, but Jim has nothing hazy or indeterminate about him. He came home at one A.M., after working the late shift at a paper mill, but woke me before dawn with moonshine on his mind. "I shouldn't even be talking to you," he said again as I sat blinking on the couch, but he couldn't resist a captive audience for long. Now he sits shirtless next to me and offers a lesson in economics, tracing diagrams on his open palm.

"In a normal operation," he says, "we use six eight-hundred-gallon stills—we call 'em black pots—each of which can make about a hundred gallons of moonshine. A black pot is really just a four-by-eight strip of stainless steel with its ends nailed together. You make the sides out of poplar or oak and cut a fourteen-inch hole in the top. Then you take that, set it up on cinder blocks in a shallow trench, and slide a propane burner underneath. The flames are about ten inches high, and it sounds like an engine runnin' real loud. When the mash starts boilin', you put a copper cap over the hole, seal it with some rye paste, and pipe the fumes to the doublin' keg—some folks call it a thumper— and then a two-inch copper worm. By the time the whiskey comes out, it's close to 200 proof and flowing about as fast as the faucet on your sink. You put that stuff in your car and it'll run it."

A tractor rumbles past on the dirt road below the house, though in the morning's foreshortening silence it sounds much closer. Jim steps quickly to one side of the living room window, peers through it obliquely for a moment, and then returns to the couch. "The name of the game is speed," he continues. "The faster you can ferment the mash, the faster you can make money, and the less chance you'll get caught. So you ferment and boil the mash in the same pot. While you're runnin' one still, you're already heatin' up the next one and adding new ingredients to what's left of your last— what they call the backin's, or sour mash."

The recipe Jim uses is 75 or 80 percent sugar— about four hundred pounds per pot—along with corn- meal or horse feed, malt, and Fleischmann's yeast. The resulting "sugar liquor" isn't quite as smooth as his father's corn liquor, but Jim can't afford to be an epicure. "It takes us about a week to get the operation set up and workin' perfect and about three weeks to work it. We run two stills a day, four runs per still.

Then we mix the runs together in a barrel, get it down to around 100 proof, and put it in those gallon milk jugs. Most of the time it's out of the state the same day."

At first the facts and figures have a hard time seeping in. My mind is still cloudy from sleep and clogged with half-remembered nightmares—of guns being put to my head; of a silent, grim-faced circle of bootleggers waiting in the forest. But Jim, I know, is nothing like those men. He speaks quickly and accurately, in a voice like honey mixed with seltzer— more crisp and dry than an east Virginia drawl has any right to be. His hazel eyes are small, watchful, and unclouded by resentment; his beard is trim and well kept; and even after a night's sleep, his short black hair lies molded to his scalp, as if gripped by an invisible skullcap. Years in the military have given his body a lean, knobby look, and he sits with a certain stiffness, as if watching himself from a slight distance, constantly correcting his posture. "I like to live my life wide open," he says, and at first this seems almost comically inapt—I've rarely met someone so guarded, so calculating. But then I think that by "wide open" he means open to any possibility, and that much, certainly, is true.

Seen in retrospect, Jim's life has been like a bumper-car ride with the pedal always to the floor: full of drive and nervy self-confidence, but marked by jolting, split-second redirections. The first bump he hit was of a genetic kind: He was born severely color-blind, unable to distinguish between a red and a blue, though he does perceive color after a fashion. The next bump was clerical: Despite the fact that she was married, his mother chose to give him her maiden name—a reminder, perhaps, that he shouldn't always follow in his father's footsteps.

There wasn't a time in Jim's life when Willard wasn't involved in moonshine—either making it, hauling it, or selling it—and on at least three occasions he was arrested for it. The first raid Jim can recall was when he was seven or eight years old. There were sheriffs and deputies all through the house, and his mother was sitting with him at the kitchen table, explaining what was going on. When she was done, Jim reached under the sink, picked up a gallon jug of moonshine that the police had overlooked, and carried it calmly through the crowd to his bedroom. Then he hid it in the toy box that his father had made for him.

Like Willard, Jim can do almost anything with his hands: weld a still, construct a house, rebuild an engine. And like Willard, he joined the army when he was eighteen, hoping to put his mechanical gifts to use. Unfortunately, the army had other ideas. They had no need for a color-blind mechanic, they said. How would he tell the differences among wires? So they shuttled him off to southern Germany to study military intelligence. "It was just a desk job," he says.

"Followin' paper trails, findin' out what was bein' bought that shouldn't be bought, rattin' on people. But it taught me how the system works, and that comes in handy with moonshinin'."

Jim rose steadily up the ranks, from corporal to lieutenant to captain, earning commendations at every step. A month after Kelly turned eighteen, he married her and brought her to Germany. By the time Desert Storm was gathering, he hoped to be among the first to fly to the Middle East, perhaps staying on for a full career in the military after that.

Then came word from his father: His mom had suffered a stroke and had less than a year to live. Jim was needed back home. "Me and Jimmy, it was the same thing," Willard told me. "I wanted to fight in Korea, like he wanted to fight in Saudi Arabia, but I got a hardship discharge, too. Had to come home and take care of my father. Same damn thing: hung between loyalty to your country and loyalty to your parents."

It was back home, living in an old trailer and watching his friends march to Kuwait on TV, that Jim fell into moonshining. Perhaps it was unavoidable, living where he did, with his father still in the business and good money to be made. Or maybe he needed some sort of adventure, some keen risk to compensate for the war he wasn't fighting. At first, he says, he considered going over to the other side— joining a SWAT team or the revenuers themselves.

But their uniforms must have been a little too close to home. So he started setting up stills instead.

—

Special agent Gerald Joyce swings his van into a narrow country road and slows to an easy, drifting pace. "That's the place," he says, jerking his chin toward a white, one-story farmhouse. "The source said it was in a tobacco barn, at the back end of the property." Behind him all banter suddenly ceases. The other members of the moonshine task force scrutinize the roadside through tinted glass.

"He said there'd be pumpkins, didn't he?"

"Yeah, a wagonload of pumpkins and a two-ton Dodge pickup truck."

"Well, there are the pumpkins, anyway." Joyce continues to the next section road and turns right, slowing to a crawl as he scans the landscape. At fifty he's the oldest member of the task force and the only one in civilian clothes. He makes a natural front man, with his graying temples and square-rimmed glasses, jowly cheeks, and smooth, articulate manner, and on days like today he's happy to be the designated driver. "I like raiding stills," he says. "But I don't like creepin' out there in the bushes during hunting season. Some of these guys will shoot at anything that moves." The others are already hustling into their gear: camouflage jackets and overalls, billy clubs and forty-caliber Beretta automatics. J. E. Calhoun, who joined the group soon after the Smith Mountain bust, glances at my burgundy T-shirt and red sneakers: "You expectin' to do some runnin', boy?" I glance up at him, wide-eyed.

"It's been several people shot wearin' red," Bev Whitmer explains, handing me his camouflage jacket. "They say it looks like a wild turkey's neck."

After a quick conference with Jimmy Beheler, the group's leader, Joyce decides to drop us off about a half mile to the side of the farm, where we can hike in unobserved. Calhoun grins up at them as he checks his walkie-talkie: "Once the two brains formulate what to do, they stop and throw our asses out."

"We're just the worker bees," Whitmer adds.

"The low men on the totem pole."

Beheler turns and glowers. His drooping mustache and duckbill hat, sullen, watery eyes, and low, grumbling voice make him look like an old, ornery hound snapping at some unruly pups: "Let's get ready to move."

It's been twelve years since Beheler started the task force, and in that time it has become the most successful group of its kind in the nation. That fact has hardly made him a local hero, however. Moonshiners may have the most violent history of any group in the country, yet it's a peculiar fact that Americans seem incapable of harboring bad feelings toward them. Homemade liquor has been illegal, off and on, for more than two centuries, but the courts still go easy on those who make it. Though it can be as addictive and debilitating as most drugs, few think to call it one. Alone among the old vices I've revisited, moonshine still claims a place in our cultural inheritance, though it long ago ceased to be quaint, or traditional, or even well made. In Franklin County moonshine memoirs fill the local paperback racks, the convenience stores sell moonshining T-shirts, and a county fair isn't complete without its copper-pot still. For a while, a local businessman even put up a billboard that declared Franklin County the "Moonshine Capital of the World."

Beheler's task force gets its share of tip-offs from ex-wives, jealous rivals, and disgruntled relations. But when most people get word, or whiff, of a still, they keep mum. The thirty-six-pot operation at Smith Mountain Lake had 150 mobile homes within eight hundred yards of it, Calhoun estimates, yet only one man bothered to report the smell. Even the local Baptist ministers tend to wink more often than thunder. "Some of these moonshiners make real good-quality stuff," one of them told me. "And if you follow Scripture straight, it does say, 'Take a little wine for your stomach's sake.'"

Beheler's best answer to such apathy is a dogged work ethic and a love of the chase. Because moonshiners tend to distill during the day and deliver at night, the task force is on call twenty-four hours a day, and there's no such thing as a weekend. One

Saturday morning about ten years ago, Beheler was driving in the country with his eleven-year-old son when he stumbled on two men running a still. "I just bailed out of the truck and told my son to stay right there," he remembers. "I ended up catching both those guys."

———

Jim will never get caught that easily—or so he says. From the very beginning he has done things differently from his father. Old-timers like Willard always lived like paupers, if only to keep from raising suspicions. They might have $150,000 in the bank yet live in a shack and drive a pickup with one door missing. Jim had no patience for that. He took a full-time job as a maintenance man at the mill and built a fully equipped, two-bay mechanic's garage behind his house. He tried his hand at corn farming and raising hogs. He scattered his hundred acres with fragments of his daydreams—tractor parts, still caps, a trailer concession stand, and dozens of used cars—and year by year he cobbled together a life from them, testing it constantly for speed, power, and reliability.

Moonshine has never been more than a side business for him, though a lucrative one. He sets up a still once a year in the fall, runs it for a month or so, and then dismantles it, keeping the copper cap and worm for the next go-round. The materials for six black pots will run him about $2,000 and the ingredients to fill them about $1,200. (He buys his sugar wholesale, in large pallets from the local SAM'S Club—"Them high school kids never ask any questions.") He'll usually hire two still hands, at $125 a day, and a cook at $200 a day, and together they'll produce around two thousand gallons of liquor before they're done. In the end he'll net around $10,000 for about 120 hours of work—about six times the hourly rate he gets at the textile plant.

The real profits, of course, lie further up the food chain. Jim may sell his liquor at the still site for $15 a gallon, but the distributor sells it to the shot houses for $30, and the customers there pay $1 a shot. "'Course, you can make the most if you own it, and haul it, and sell it yourself. But I don't need that kind of risk," Jim says. So he doesn't even know the men who haul away his liquor. "They just show up with an empty truck, we fill it up, and the cycle starts over again."

—

Agent Joyce brings the van to a sudden, grinding stop, Calhoun flings open the sliding door, and everyone barrels down the embankment. For just a moment we huddle in the shade of a pine tree to get our bearings, then we veer off into the forest in single file. According to Joyce, the tobacco barn in question has a shiny new chain and lock, some freshly cut sticks by the door, and a stash of moonshine inside. But there are no barns in sight yet, only acres of thorny bottomland.

"This is gonna be fun."

"And we ain't got but a quarter of an hour to get through it."

Calhoun flips his hat around backward and surges into the brambles with a grunt. To guarantee a conviction, they not only have to catch their man red-handed, they have to physically restrain him—juries don't always trust an agent's eyes, and alibis are easy to come by. Over the years they've all suffered their share of lacerations and bruises, poked eyes and twisted knees, from stalking, chasing, and wrestling moonshiners. Beheler once needed eighteen stitches after running headlong into a barbed-wire fence during a raid. But no one here has ever been shot. Possessing firearms at the scene of a crime carries a much stiffer penalty than making moonshine, so most bootleggers do without them. And though the agents carry guns, firing at a fleeing bootlegger is out of the question. "I wouldn't even carry this damn heavy thing," Calhoun says, patting his Beretta, "if it weren't for the possibility of a booby trap." The gun that comes in most handy, Beheler adds, is loaded with BBs: "Keeps the dogs quiet."

We work our way through a patch of bloodred sumac, the greenbriers catching at our clothes as we pass. After a few hundred yards we reach a winding creek, thick with algae, and then a steep slope that leads to an airy grove of white oak. It's a cool autumn day, with clouds racing across the sun, but by the

time we reach the back side of the house, I'm
sweating beneath my fatigues. Crouching to catch
our breath, we agree to split into two groups.
Whitmer peels off to follow a path into the woods,
while the rest of us pass through a small stand of
pines and across a meadow covered with spindly
black stalks of ragweed. A deeply rutted road skirts it
on the other side. "Too rough for a car," Calhoun
says, looking down. "But a four-wheeler could make
it."

By now there are tobacco barns every hundred yards
or so, and we begin to check them one by one. At first
no one says a word, and we slink around as delicately
as cats, prying open doors, peering under tarps, and
squinting through chinks in the barns' wooden walls.
At one point Calhoun sees me walking down the
center of the road and shoos me to the side, then
walks over and scuffs away my footprints. Still, after
half a dozen empty barns, even his commando form
starts to go slack. When Whitmer rejoins us, his
slumped shoulders tell the same story: no shiny new
lock and chain, no fresh tobacco sticks, no booze.

"Well, well, well."

"I think this is what's known in the business as a
dead end."

Beheler spits in the bushes. Then he calls Joyce on
his walkie-talkie, and we head back toward the road.
Four out of five leads end up this way, I know. But
there's an odd feeling, when you've been running

around in the woods with funny clothes on for no reason, that you've been the butt of an elaborate practical joke. Moonshining is a cat-and-mouse game, everyone says, but it feels suddenly as if we're the mice: camouflaged like forest animals, skulking around in the underbrush, trespassing on private property.

Even Calhoun, standing there with his linebacker's build and Beretta automatic, is more vulnerable than he seems. He's spent his whole life in this area, and a good chunk of it crawling through the woods as a game warden or special agent. He knows the moonshiners' faces and their family histories, the cars they drive and the bars they frequent. But then they know him just as well.

Earlier that morning Jim took me out for a drive. About five miles from his house, he suddenly pulled up in front of a small ranch house with a silver trailer beside it. "You know who lives here?" he asked, smiling impishly. "Man by the name of Calhoun." He pointed to the front door and asked, half-jokingly, if we should leave him a note. Then, like a dog marking his territory, he drove up the driveway and spun around, spraying gravel from his back wheels as he left.

—

Moonshiners have always had to be stealthier than drug dealers; their product is so much bulkier, their manufacturing methods so much more complicated and conspicuous. But in recent years, prodded by groups like Beheler's, they've had to modernize their methods. When helicopters began to scan the forest, moonshiners camouflaged their stills with maple-leaf stencils. When motorboats puttered down streams in search of wood fires and exposed water pumps, moonshiners switched to propane and submersible pumps. When agents prowled the woods with infrared scopes, night-vision goggles, and motion-detecting cameras, moonshiners got the same equipment.

These days the biggest stills have moved indoors—whether in tobacco barns, chicken houses, or purpose-built structures—where water and heat are easy to come by. They're often hidden underground or behind false walls, and they may pump their liquor to a separate, inconspicuous building for loading. (A few years ago a still in northern Georgia was found in a basement, at the bottom of a hidden staircase. When you turned on the tap upstairs, moonshine came out.) But all those advances have come at a cost: moonshining, once the quintessential egalitarian enterprise, open to any hardworking man with a few dollars, now has its own class system.

"The big operators have brick houses," Jim tells me one morning, walking around his place, waiting for another moonshiner to arrive. "They drive Mercedes. They have doctor's degrees. They've got, like, different lives." He stops and picks at the scorched remains of his mother's house, a few yards behind his trailer. "Now, this guy you're gonna meet, he's at the other end of it: he's a still hand. He doesn't even have electricity in his house, and he likes to live that way. He's like a modern bum."

There's something odd in the way Jim says this—as if he were shamed by it rather than amused—but I chalk it up to empathy later, when I meet the man. He sits on Jim's deck, eyes blinking in the sun, looking like a cross between Wild Bill Hickok and a forest gnome. He has a caved-in chest and shaky hands, shoulder-length hair, a scraggly mustache, and features flushed and bludgeoned by drink. His eyes are pale green, rimmed with black, his eyelids always at half-mast, and when he talks his tongue darts behind broken teeth, as if looking for a place to hide. He says his name is Leroy and that he's forty-eight years old, though he looks closer to sixty-five. He says he won't say anything about the living, but he's happy to talk about the dead. "You can't do nothin' to them."

From the time he was twelve years old, Leroy has made moonshine. He started out by toting sacks of sugar and scouting for signs of revenuers, then graduated to tending the still. He'd get up at three in the morning to light the fire and heat the mash, then head over to Zenith Junior High for classes. "My parents didn't know where I was; didn't care, I guess." His real father, you might say, was his boss: Aubrey Atkins, "Kingfish of the Franklin County Moonshiners," who would later teach Jim as well.

Aubrey was a rhinoceros of a man, only five feet nine but more than 230 pounds, with a single-minded love of moonshining. He was deaf in one ear and tended to bellow more than talk, and his irrepressible spirit—and above-average product—endeared him even to some judges. When the moonshining exhibit was built at Smith Mountain Lake, Aubrey was the only living moonshiner it showed, though by then he looked like a man from another age.

Over the years Aubrey put Leroy through a cooking school as exacting as Escoffier and an advanced course on camouflage as well. One of his favorite tricks was to cut down a few young pine trees and plant them like Christmas trees across the path leading to a still. Whenever a moonshiner arrived, he'd simply pull out the trees, drive on through, and then stick them back in the ground. "The first time I got caught in a raid I was just seventeen," Leroy says, "and everyone kinda left me there, with agents comin' in from every side. Well, I just ran over to a brush pile and pulled all them little pine trees over me. I must've laid there three hours, while they were bustin' things up. They never did find me."

As savvy as Aubrey was, his age and outdated methods eventually caught up with him. By his late sixties he'd lost a step or two to the agents he used to outrun, and the task force arrested him three times. In the end, the man who had outrun countless revenuers in the woods, who'd begun moonshining before the war and survived to the age of seventy-two, was caught short by a couple of teenage robbers with a shotgun. It took two blasts to kill him, Leroy says, and then his body was so heavy that they could drag it only two hundred yards off the road. A few days later a police helicopter spotted his shallow grave in the hard winter soil.

The killers are now serving extended sentences in the state penitentiary. But Leroy would rather not think about that. He'd rather think about the last time Aubrey was raided, when they were still together. "I'd just bruised my chest in an accident, so I couldn't run," he says. "But Aubrey, he just jumped over the top of that eight-hundred-gallon pot and ran right into the pines. They was yellin', 'Aubrey, we know who you is!' But he couldn't hear 'em, so he just ran on. I mean, it was like Alley Oop goin' through the jungle: you could hear the pines a-poppin'."

He hunches over then, as if in pain, his shoulders convulsing. I start to comfort him, then realize he's only laughing—a great soundless laugh, with his features bunching together as if someone had pulled a drawstring inside his skull. It's a startling sight, but after a while I can't help laughing along. "Oh man," he says, rubbing his right eye. "I wish I had me a jug of that moonshine right now."

—

Later I watch through the back window as Leroy helps Jim and his father dig a drainage ditch with a backhoe.

Beside me, Kelly is sautéing some cabbage for lunch, keeping an eye on Audie, who's bent on cutting the kitchen table in half with his toy saw. Short and stoutly built, with curly brown tresses, a little girl's bangs, and a voice that rarely drops below a bray, Kelly seems as sweet tempered and uncomplicated as a Clydesdale. But when I ask her about Leroy, her eyes cloud over. "He's worthless," she says. "I know he's Jim's brother and all, but if Jim were anything like him, I wouldn't have him."

I stare at her blankly for a moment: Jim told me that they weren't related. "Well, he's his adopted brother, actually," she says. Then she jabs a finger at Jim's mom's cabin. "That's where he grew up."

Like most people in Franklin County, Kelly has her own deep history with moonshine. Her father was a great lover of it, though he never set up a still himself. "He was a real violent drunk," she says, "and my mama took a lot of licks to protect the kids. One time, I remember, she threw a big butcher's knife at him, and it stuck in the wood next to his head and just vibrated." She stops and looks up from the sizzling pan, the spatula suspended in midair. Then she continues in the same matter-of-fact voice. "He died in a car wreck when I was six," she says. "Took the top of his head clean off."

I ask if Jim's moonshining frightens her, and she says it does sometimes, especially now that Audie's around, but she tries not to think about it.

Outside, the others are hunkered down together in the ditch they've dug: Jim, giving orders and gesturing around the yard; Willard, already flushed from a few nips at his flask of Virginia Lightning; Leroy, looking surprisingly sturdy with his shirt off, his shoulders tanned and corded from years of outdoor work. While they talk, Audie squirts through the back door and careens toward them, waving a screwdriver. Before they notice, he's climbed into the ditch beside his father, only a few feet from the backhoe's gaping metal jaws. "Jim!" Kelly shouts through the window. But he just smiles and waves, climbing back into the driver's seat. As he guns the engine, Audie settles in next to his grandfather and starts to dig. In his element at last.

—

The bulletin board behind Jimmy Beheler's desk is crowded with yellowed newspaper clippings and curling snapshots. Though the backgrounds vary, the scenes are always the same: five barrel-chested men in camouflage, chopping up stills or posing in front of them, smiling for the camera like hunters with their kill. "Crime Does Pay," a bright red bumper sticker above the board declares, ironically. But when I ask Beheler about it today, he shakes his head. "Sad but true," he says. "Sad but true."

He's having a bad year. Though the task force will end up destroying some five thousand gallons of moonshine this year, that's only 1/200th of the illicit liquor produced in the area. And though they'll bust thirty-six stills—seven times as many as all the agents in Georgia put together—that's still a far cry from the hundred they busted in 1993. "I don't know," Calhoun says, leaning back and scratching his stomach. "We're doing the same things, but we aren't catchin' 'em as much as we used to. Which leads me to think that they must have changed the way they do business."

What galls Beheler's crew most isn't that some moonshiners get away, but that they get away even when they've been caught. Possession of moonshine is only a misdemeanor in Virginia, whether it involves a gallon in the backseat or a thousand gallons in the trailer. And although making moonshine is a felony, most first offenders get off with a small fine. "They'll play that romantic, Depression-era thing to death," Joyce says. "You'll see him one day all slicked up, driving a $30,000 vehicle to pick up his girl for steak and lobster. The next day he's a hillbilly without a pot to pee in." A local man by the name of Elmo Bridges was arrested twenty-four times for making moonshine, yet he never spent more than a few months in jail.

Beheler says it doesn't get to him anymore—"You do what you can do, you do the best you can do, and that's all you can do"—but his mood, and frequent talk of retirement, suggest differently. Today he takes off early to play a round of golf, but the others stay behind a while longer, mulling over the empty afternoon, reluctant to emerge from their funk. They crack a few jokes about Randall Toney, the fifth member of the crew, who's off today. They talk about the economics of moonshine and how it often destroys those who most profit from it. They agree that it's nasty stuff, but that in eighteen years they've confiscated only a handful of dangerous batches. Then Joyce reaches under his desk and pulls out a half-gallon mason jar filled with white lightning. "We got this a few weeks ago," he says, unscrewing the lid and handing me the jar. "Go ahead," he says. "Taste it."

—

Moonshine, I've been told more than once by now, is just another word for poison. A hundred years ago, perhaps, some people made it the way they made fine furniture. But what pride it involved, what craft, was all but dismantled by Prohibition. As demand skyrocketed, some moonshiners began to throw lye, sulfuric acid, car batteries, or sacks of steaming manure into the mash to hasten fermentation. They cut their product with bleach, turpentine, rubbing alcohol, or paint thinner; stained it with tobacco juice or iodine. They cooked it in galvanized steel or distilled it in car radiators that gave off lead from soldered parts.

A few of the moonshiners I talked to said these were nothing but scare stories, passed around by revenuers. But others admitted that there have always been two sorts of moonshine: the decent stuff, which is kept at home and sold to neighbors, and "nigger likker," as they called it, shipped to anonymous shot houses and nip joints in the big city. It's in such areas that moonshine has taken its worst toll. In 1928 sixty died of wood alcohol poisoning in New York alone, and in 1930 authorities estimated that fifteen thousand people had been partially paralyzed by "Jake," a type of moonshine made with Jamaica ginger. "Buyin' moonshine is like playin' Russian roulette," Willard told me. "It won't hurt ya if it's good—I mean, you can drink that white lightnin' and go to work the next day. But the bad stuff, it's a killer."

Even a few sips of Jake, I tell myself, wouldn't be enough to hurt me. But even so, as I lift up Joyce's jar, I feel like a kid in high school again, buckling under peer pressure. At first all I can sense are the fumes burning through my sinuses. Then, little by little, the air clears, and the taste that lingers is clean, sweet, and surprisingly mild, with a faint afterglow of formaldehyde. "Not bad," I say just to get their goat.

For a beat or two they exchange glances, and the room's pulse seems to quicken. "Shut the door," Whitmer says, opening a file cabinet beside him. And then, suddenly, it's as if I'm back at the moonshiners' reunion and the 'shine tasting has just been announced. From every drawer and cardboard box, it seems, mason jars start popping out, as if the room were full of jack-in-the-boxes. Jars of damson plum and jars of peach; jars of cherry moonshine and more jars of white lightning: the essence and fruit, perfectly preserved, of years of tailing moonshiners.

Joyce passes me a half gallon of liquor so purple it's nearly opaque. The taste is deep and musky and sweetly familiar. "Blackberry," he says, grinning. Then a jar of liquid sunshine emerges, eight pears bobbing happily inside it, and soon Joyce is telling us about the charcoal keg his father used to own. Calhoun remembers a still they once busted that smelled just like Jack Daniel's, and Whitmer reminisces some more about the Smith Mountain bust. "Do you have any connections to Hollywood?" he wants to know. "'Cause we're thinkin' of getting us some agents. I'm thinkin' about Stallone for my part."

"I'd be happy with Sean Connery," Joyce adds.

"'Course, Randall Toney, he'll have to be played by Tony Randall."

That breaks them up for a while: three big men in a tiny room, surrounded by mason jars of every color, imagining themselves in those actors' bodies, chasing down some hapless local citizen. And for a moment the retirement plans and lenient courts are forgotten, and moonshine seems like only a game again— neither poison nor birthright nor cynical livelihood, just an excuse for grown men to play hide-and-seek in the woods.

"You know what I remember best?" Calhoun says,

wiping his eyes. "It isn't all the adventure or the busts, it's the funny stuff. The ridiculous situations you get into."

"Like the time that copperhead crawled over Butch Wright's foot and he killed it with his umbrella."

"Or the time Garry Thomas came with us."

"Gerald, tell him about Garry."

Joyce looks away for a second, his eyes fixed on some middle distance in his memory. "Well," he begins, "you have to know Garry to get it. I mean, he's the nicest guy in the world, but he's from the city and he's never worked liquor before, and he keeps buggin' us all the time to take him on a raid. He just has this thing about wantin' to bust moonshiners.

"So one day we're working and watching this place with Garry, when a truck comes by with a bunch of barrels in the back. Jimmy and Randall are close by, so they run up to it. But those guys must have seen 'em comin', 'cause the truck pulls away and goes up a gravel road and into a field. The guys inside just jump out and run."

"Turns out the barrels are full of spent mash."

"Now, you've got to understand that spent mash is about the sorriest-smellin' stuff in the world. Fresh mash may smell like a loaf of bread, but spent mash smells like a pigpen. So naturally someone asks Garry if he wants to taste it. 'No,' he says, he doesn't want to taste the mash. But he'll take the truck and drive it in." Joyce takes a breath and grins at the others, rolling the jar of pears between his hands. "Now, Garry, to get back to the road, he has to drive all the way around this field. But when he comes back toward us, there's somethin' wrong."

"The field's wet, and his brakes aren't workin'."

"So he's goin' faster and faster, and he can't stop. He hits the front fender of one of the police cars, and then he about runs over my toes. He goes all the way to the bottom, the truck bouncin' this way and that, and then he smashes into a ditch.

"Well, that's when the truck stops, but those barrels of mash in back, they just keep on goin': right through the back window and all over Garry.

"The rest of us, we're kind of in shock. We run up and say, 'Garry, are you okay? Are you okay?' And he says he is. But I mean, he's just covered in that mash. There are clumps of it in his hair and it's all over his face and it's dripping down his shirt into his pants. So we're all just starin' at him, kinda dumbstruck. And then someone breaks the silence: 'Garry,' he says, 'I didn't think you wanted to taste the mash.'"

"Jimmy, he laughed so hard, he peed in his pants."

"I about hyperventilated myself."

Joyce grins. "If we could just have been a little more quiet," he says, "I swear we would have heard the moonshiners laughin', too."

Mad Squirrels and Kentuckians

A September dawn, windless and clear, with the sky going to lavender behind the high branches. At the bottom of a hollow, Steve Rector and I wind our way along an ocher creek bed, stepping slowly from rock to rock to avoid the crackling leaves. These beeches should still be cloaked in emerald so early in the season, this creek overflowing its banks, but western Kentucky is in the throes of perhaps the worst drought in half a century. The one puddle in sight has been claimed by a box turtle, and camouflage clothes are our only cover.

Rector crouches down ahead of me, balancing his sixteen-gauge Winchester on his shoulder, and comes up with a handful of broken shells: beechnuts, gnawed open by little mouths. "I came through here on Sundee, but there wasn't any cuttin's at all," he whispers, moving on. In the distance a woodpecker's hammering dopplers through the forest. Using his shotgun as a crutch, Rector tries to clamber up the bank, but his feet slip just as his body goes horizontal. He reaches for a sapling, but it isn't there, and all three hundred pounds of him come crashing down at once. For a moment he just lies in the dirt, his basset-hound features looking more than usually defeated. "Well," he says, groaning back to his feet, "I guess I must have that mad-cow disease after all."

How many other squirrel hunters, I wonder, are thinking the same thing this morning? The epidemic that killed fifty-six people in Britain and has sent almost three million cows to the incinerator is half a continent and ocean away. No American cow has died of mad-cow disease, or bovine spongiform encephalopathy, and British beef has never found a market here. Still, panic has a way of finding new victims.

In August of 1997 two neurologists, Joseph Berger and Eric Weisman, both recent transplants to Kentucky, published an odd letter in the British medical journal *The Lancet*. A disturbing pattern had come to their attention, they wrote. In the previous four years, five patients in west Kentucky had been diagnosed with Creutzfeldt-Jakob disease, or CJD, of which mad-cow disease is a variant. All five patients had one trait in common: they ate squirrel brains. Given that some forms of CJD can be transmitted by the eating of infected brains, and that most mammals seem able to carry the disease, the connection made sense. "Caution might be exercised," the authors concluded, "in the ingestion of this arboreal rodent."

To a country primed for the next epidemic, this was perversely welcome news. As the terror of AIDS slowly subsided in America, fears of future viruses were beginning to flare up. Books like *The Coming Plague*, *The Hot Zone*, and *Deadly Feasts* were joining best-seller lists, and disease movies weren't far behind. Now here was the perfect fuel for all that smoldering paranoia. Mad-squirrel disease, if it existed, was as fatal and as exotic as any novelist could wish, yet most people were no more likely to get it than the plague. If AIDS once seemed an affliction cooked up by country Baptists to punish city dwellers, here was the urbanites' revenge: a disease, common only among squirrel-brain-eating hillbillies, that turned its victims into demented fools. What could be more appropriate?

The feeding frenzy was brief but exceedingly gleeful. *The New York Times* began by garnishing the story with some suitably gothic details. "Families that eat brains follow only certain rituals," the paper reported, then it quoted Eric Weisman: "Someone comes by the house with just the head of a squirrel and gives it to the matriarch of the family. She shaves the fur off the top of the head and fries the head whole. The skull is cracked open at the dinner table and the brains are sucked out." Squirrels recently killed on the road, the *Times* added, "are often thrown into the pot." Soon Jay Leno and David Letterman were riffing on squirrel brains in their monologues, and columnists across the country were chiming in. "This report raises some troubling questions," wrote syndicated humorist Dave Barry. "1. Since when do squirrels have brains? 2. Have squirrels and cows been mating? How? 3. Doesn't a person who eats road kill rodent organs pretty much deserve to die?"

Steve Rector first heard about it in the coffee room at work. He was putting some squirrel heads into the microwave for lunch, he remembers, when one of the guys mentioned the mad-cow-disease story in the Owensboro paper. "I figured that if it was really bad, like the bubonic plague, it would be on TV," Rector says. So he started to watch the evening news, scan the local obituaries, and look for signs of strange behaviour in local squirrels. Though he didn't see or hear anything more, he was spooked enough to lay off brains for the first time in thirty years. But that was last year. Like most of the squirrel hunters I met, he couldn't stay away for long. "I just thought, You gotta die of somethin'," he says. "First it was cigarettes cause cancer, then pesticides, and then the water you drink. But I been eatin' squirrel brains since I was six years old, and I ain't dead yet."

It's midmorning now, and our vest pockets have yet to hold any dead squirrels. But as we circle back to

the truck, Rector stops suddenly and gestures for me
to hang back. Peering at the crest of a distant hill, he
slowly raises his shotgun to his shoulder and shoots
twice in quick succession, the reports ripping the air
around me. Then he hustles up the slope toward a
skinny maple tree.

Rector is no champion marksman. At forty-four he
has developed astigmatism and can't use a rifle
without a scope. He reflexes have slowed down, his
heart beats irregularly, and his fingers go numb in the
morning cold. Yet when he reaches the tree, his face
breaks into a boyish grin. "That was a hell of a shot,"
he says, "sixty yards if anything." Reaching into the
leaf litter, he pulls out a young squirrel, its tiny chest
still heaving. "Smell of 'im," he says almost tenderly,
lifting the warm body to my nose. "Isn't that just like
. . . the woods?" Then he takes the animal by the tail
and beats its head methodically against the tree.
"Don't want to do that too hard," he says after a
couple of whacks. "Else I'll spoil the best part."

—

If hunters around here seem uncommonly suspicious
of authority (medical or otherwise); if they clamp on
to their traditions even at peril of their lives, they
have good reason. Ninety years ago, when Rector's
father's father was cutting the giant scaly-bark
hickories out of these bottomlands and rafting them
to the mill, it was said that the land would make its
people rich. But eastern land speculators reaped

most of the timber and mining profits, and a tobacco monopoly took what was left. When the virgin forests were gone, Rector's grandfather went to work as a sharecropper and then a coal miner, and when his son turned twenty-two, he joined them.

Miners back then dug vertical shafts two hundred feet down and up to four miles long, with thin wooden props and little ventilation. They used black powder to blast out the coal and steel picks to chop it up, praying that their carbide lamps wouldn't ignite a pocket of gas. After as many as seventeen hours underground, they emerged black as crows and got paid in company scrip, redeemable only at company stores. The results was best summed up by Merle Travis, whose father and brothers worked in the same mine as Rector's mother's father:

> *You load sixteen tons and what do you get?*
> *Another day older and deeper in debt*
> *St. Peter, don't you call me 'cause I can't go*
> *I owe my soul to the company store.*

When Rector was a little boy, and a life underground seemed his inevitable lot, he used to have a recurring dream. He was standing on a high hill overlooking a strip mine, waiting for his father to drive by so he could wave to him. Far below, the mine pit had filled with rain, and the acids in the coal had turned the water bright blue. "I was always wearin' a red shirt and blue jeans, and every time I'd just fall off that edge toward that Bahama blue water," he says. "I'm terrible scared of heights, and I'm not too good a swimmer, so I swear that fall took forever."

In his dream, Rector always woke up before he hit the water. But in real life it was the coal business itself that saved him. "Don't bother," the owner told his father when he went looking for a job for his son. "The mines are almost played out. You're better off lettin' that boy finish high school." So Rector took a job as a meat cutter at a supermarket, while his father stayed on at the mine. His father's father died of consumption eventually, exacerbated by black-lung disease. "The last two years of his life he had to sleep sittin' up in a chair," Rector says. "Couldn't get his breath otherwise."

Eventually, Rector got married, had a son, and was promoted to meat manager at the supermarket. "I had a forty-acre farm, a brand-new house, and a brand-new Crown Victoria car," he says. But then, eleven years ago, his wife left him, and he was back where he started. To keep up with alimony and child-support payments, he took a union job at the power plant, shovelling coal ashes with a front-end loader.

He has since remarried and moved to a small and nondescript ranch house—"a plain old country house," as he puts it—just off Paradise Street, in the town of Greenville, in Muhlenberg County. To a fan of folk music, staying there is something like staying

at the Heartbreak Hotel. It constantly brings to mind
the refrain of a song:

> *And Daddy, won't you take me back to*
> *Muhlenberg County*
> *Down by the Green River where Paradise lay?*
> *Well, I'm sorry, my son, but you're too late in*
> *asking*
> *Mr. Peabody's coal train has hauled it away.*

—

There are three things that every Rector man has
always done, an oral historian once told Steve: hunt,
make moonshine, and play guitar. Rector never did
take to moonshining (maybe it was seeing his great-
uncle's pajamas with the small hole in front, where
the bullet went in, and the giant hole in back, where
it came out). But he more than makes up for it with
his other hobbies. In a county that calls itself the
"Thumb-Picking Capital of the World," his command
of the guitar has earned him an honorary street sign,
and his love of hunting is nearly as legendary. At the
age of six he went hunting with his daddy, carrying a
BB gun to kill crippled squirrels. At ten he had his
own shotgun. "And then pretty soon I was huntin' all
the time."

In New York or Boston, where squirrels eat hand-
outs and scamper impudently above park benches,
squirrel hunting can seem like poor sport. But in
Kentucky squirrels know the meaning of fear. The

leap to the canopy at the first sign of movement. They baa to one another, like lambs on speed, sounding the alarm. They flatten their bodies against trees, rotating slowly to keep the trunk between them and the hunter, or just dive into the nearest knothole. "I'd say they're pretty damn smart," Rector says. "I don't know how many pairs of my socks I've burned up trying to smoke 'em out."

Rector's father taught him a few squirrel-hunting tricks, but most of what he knows he learned from his cousin Jimmy Vincent. Tall, skinny, and agile as an otter, Jimmy was nine years older than Steve and half orphaned by the state: his father was in prison for killing a man. When Jimmy was ten years old, another boy shot him in the right eye with a BB gun. ("It didn't bust it," Rector says. "It just went behind the eyeball so he couldn't see with it anymore—it had a funny shine to it, like it was made of glass.") But Jimmy didn't let that stop him. He simply learned to aim over his left shoulder, and killed more squirrels with one eye than most did with two.

"Jimmy was like the Chet Atkins of squirrel hunting," Rector says. "He had a sixth sense about 'em. He could smell 'em through the leaves." If the woods went suddenly quiet, Jimmy would pick up a nut and scratch it with his pocketknife—an all-clear sign to the squirrels. If a knothole was within reach, he'd cut a cross in the end of a green stick, poke it in the hole, and twist until it got caught in some hair;

then he'd pull out the squealing animal. If a squirrel was hiding on the far side of a tree, he'd tie a string to a sapling and shake it on one side and wait for the squirrel to circle around to the other. "Back when I hunted with my daddy, he used to just say, "Walk around there, boy, and check that bush,'" Rector remembers. It wasn't till later that I realized he was usin' me as his string."

All through their youth, Jimmy and Steve kept the family supplied with squirrel meat. It was said, in those days, that squirrel soup could cure a cold, but its healing properties were mostly in the form of raw nutrition. What game there was in Kentucky was small, and coal company wages could pay for meat only twice a month. The two boys would get up before dawn, kill a mess of squirrels, and make it to class by seven-thirty. (In elementary school they hung the tails from their bicycle handlebars; in high school, from their car antennas.) "I remember one time Jimmy and I killed ninety-nine squirrels in a stretch of five days." Rector says. "My mom just pressure-cooked 'em all and put 'em in jars with barbecue sauce. That way, all winter long we could have squirrel sandwiches whenever we wanted."

Alien as they sound, such habits have shaped countless American boyhoods. Squirrels are usually a hunter's first kill, historian Stuart Marks writes in his book *Southern Hunting in Black and White,* and they nest in his memory ever after. "I'd rather kill me six

fox squirrels than a ten-point Boone-Crockett buck,"
Steve says, and he'd rather see a squirrel run free
than waste any part of its meat. Besides, he says, all
of it tastes good.

After our first morning of hunting, we dropped by
to see Juanita Adkins, the owner of the property we'd
been hunting on. Small and neatly put together, with
wide glasses, bright-white hair, and mischievous
eyes, Adkins is eighty-three years old but sharper
than most neuroscientists. She took up painting a few
years ago, and her farmhouse is hung with skillful oils
flanked by the blue ribbons she's won for them at
state and county fairs. Standing in her living room
and admiring her animal paintings, Rector asked her
if she'd ever eaten squirrels brains. Adkins looked at
him as if he were a little dim: "When I was growin'
up," she said, "that's all I'd ever eat was the brain."

———

There was a time, not so long ago, when neurologist
Eric Weisman would have laughed at the thought of
eating squirrel brains; a time when he would have
dismissed it as yet another puzzling local custom, in
a state that seemed to have an endless supply of
them. Then a squirrel-brain eater showed up at
Weisman's Neurobehavioral Institute in Beaver
Dam, Kentucky. And soon Weisman was asking all
his patients if they had the same habit.

At the age of fifty-four, Marvin, as I'll call him, was
still robust, articulate, and sharp enough to run his

hometown as mayor. True, he'd gotten fired from his day job recently for forgetting to fill out the left side of sales forms. And yes, he did hit that nun's car. But these were all misunderstandings, he said. For some reason he just didn't see the nun coming from the left, even though it was broad daylight. The crash didn't hurt him much—just a fender bender. But when they took him to the hospital in Bowling Green, he couldn't seem to keep from nodding off.

"They did a sleep study on him after that, but the problem didn't go away," Weisman remembers. "They said it was a stroke at first, and then a brain tumor. Then they sent him to me." In the tests that followed, an odd pattern emerged: If Weisman asked Marvin to draw a clock, for instance, he would cram all the numbers on the right side of its face. "He had what we call a nondominant-hemispheric syndrome," Weisman says. "The left side of the world just didn't exist for him." An EEG revealed a strange, periodic disturbance in Marvin's brain waves, and an MRI scan revealed that the right side of his brain had atrophied. But what was the cause? "I just didn't have a good answer," Weisman says. "And then I saw him jerk."

Some eighty years before, a German physician name Hans Gerhard Creutzfeldt had seen the same twitch in one of patients. She was a twenty-three-year-old orphan who had once cheerfully worked as a maid at a convent; now she refused to eat or bathe, grew paranoid, and assumed strange positions. And there was worse to come. Bouts of wild laughter grew into ceaseless screams; chronic tics amplified into waves of epileptic seizures; periods of stupor devolved into catatonia and finally death. When Creutzfeldt autopsied the patient's brain, he found masses of fibrous brown glial cells—designed to repair damaged tissue—spread through it like spackling on an old plaster wall.

Even today, no one knows for sure what causes such damage. Most doctors blame bits of rogue protein called prions. Others finger stealth viruses, known as virions, or insidious, corkscrew-shaped organisms known as spiroplasma. Whatever its origin, the disease that was eventually named for Creutzfeldt and his colleague, Alfons Jakob, is among the most mysterious in all neuropathology. Invariably fatal, CJD chooses victims across gender, race, class, and geographic lines. It can incubate, unseen, for decades and predominantly strikes the middle-aged and elderly. Over the years, forms of it have been found in sheep (scrapie), cows (bovine spongiform encephalopathy), and certain cannibals in New Guinea (kuru). Mad-cow disease and kuru have further been shown to infect those who eat infected meat, particularly brains. But true CJD strikes rarely and randomly, killing one person in a million. "It's like plane crashes," Weisman says, "it only seems to happen to nice people."

Not long after Marvin's first visit, his mind began to seize up with increasing violence, like an engine that first runs out of oil, then grinds down its bearings, and finally throws a rod. What had looked like hiccups gave way to full-fledged spasms, and his mental lapses spread to his whole brain. "If you said, 'With the pen touch the comb,' he could do it fine," Weisman says. "But if you said, 'Touch the comb with the pen,' he wouldn't understand." Meanwhile other patients were arriving with related symptoms. There were a few who couldn't walk straight, one with mysterious back pains, and two with full-blown dementia. Over the next five years Weisman alone treated six people in the early stages of CJD.

"I don't even like to look at those charts," Weisman says. "It makes me start crying." Yet there is something of the magpie in most neurologists— something that can't resist the odd mental disorder, the shiny fragment of a mind that somehow casts light on all of human consciousness. The coauthor of the *Lancet* paper, Joseph Berger, calls himself "a collector of unusual patients," and Oliver Sacks has made a career of the same pursuit. Weisman says he was never interested in publicity. But the eerie glow of these rare cases—cases related to a disease that was then much in the news—must have been hard to resist: will-o'-the-wisps beckoning him out of a long exile.

Born in 1957 to a Jewish family in the suburb of

Peabody, Massachusetts, Weisman had once seemed destined to become a Boston intellectual, if not a Brahmin. His father was an artist and businessman who sculpted the heads of the swan boats in the Boston Public Gardens. His mother was a soprano with a Boston Opera company. (When she retired she was replaced by her understudy, Beverly Sills. Later she went on to earn her BA in archaeology from Harvard—valedictorian at seventy-one.) By the age of six, Eric was drawing pictures of brains. By sixteen, he was taking a course in neuroanatomy at MIT.

He entered a summer program at Harvard after his junior year of high school, dreaming of becoming a brain surgeon. But when fall arrived he declined to stay on. "It was so competitive," he says. "People were stealing my research, pulling pages out of reference books so no one else could read them." He enrolled at Bard instead, started a rock band, and let his grade point slipped so low he couldn't get into an American medical school. In the end, he went to Grenada—just in time for the U.S. invasion. ("The local kids were throwing rocks at us, but we got to meet General Schwarzkopf.") Although he went on to an internship and residency in Mobile, Alabama, and a fellowship at Boston University, he had long since ceased to be a wunderkind, in 1992, when a headhunter offered him a job in a rural Kentucky, he took it.

It was in Alabama that he overheard a conversation that would change the course of his life. He was

watching Frank Bastian, the neuropathologist who
first suggested that spiroplasma cause CJD, dissect
the brain of a CJD patient. "Bastian turned to his
resident and asked him what kind of history it had,"
Weisman remembers. "Was he a farmer or a factory
worker? Did he eat sheep brains, cow brains, or pig
brains?" When he got to the last question, the
resident answered, Yes, the patient ate squirrel
brains.

—

Today, relaxing on a terrace overlooking the Ohio
River, Weisman seems at first glance to have settled
in quite nicely. His hair is long, black, and fashion-
ably unkempt, his body stocky and sunburned. While
jazz fusion pulses from massive speakers behind us,
he pads around barefoot, in khakis and a striped
cotton shirt open halfway down his chest. "I don't
know if you know, but neurologists don't usually live
like this," he says, gesturing back at his swimming
pool and deck chairs, his two-story home with its
skylit cathedral ceilings and mantelpiece hung with
an English fox-hunting scene. "Guys like me, in New
York, we usually have one-bedroom apartments."

Yet this house, breezy and sunlit as it seems, has
become a fortress of sorts, and Weisman is in a state
of siege. He may be a card-carrying member of the
Kentucky Colonels, the state's prestigious fraternal
organization, but he's been tarred and feathered by
the local press. He may have one of the finest homes

in Owensboro, but his own neighbor—an eater of squirrel brains, Weisman suspects—won't talk to him. He may be married to a former candidate for Miss Kentucky, but by now she's ready to move to Boston herself. "You aren't going to get me killed, are you?" Weisman asked the first time I called. "I've gotten death threats, you know." The next time, he answered the phone by saying, "Squirrel brains," as if uttering a secret password. When I asked him how he knew who was calling, he said he had caller ID.

All this trouble, Weisman says, all this bitterness and innuendo, is a result of good medicine and bad media. It began a year or so before Marvin died, when the other dementia patients were beginning to crop up. Marvin had mentioned that he liked to eat squirrel brains, which had reminded Weisman of Frank Bastian's CJD patient in Alabama. When Weisman mentioned this connection to Joseph Berger, who is chairman of the neurology department at the University of Kentucky Medical Center, in Lexington, it immediately struck a chord. Berger had seen a patient from Kentucky in the later 1980s, he said. That man had eaten squirrel brains, too.

Over the next few months, while Weisman went through his CJD records, Berger conducted a small survey. Out of a hundred local people, he found twenty-seven who had eaten squirrel brains. (In fact, more than three million people hunt squirrels in America, and in Kentucky, Ohio, and Tennessee alone twenty-five million squirrels are killed every year.) If the squirrel-brain connection was real, the two neurologists thought, there might be many more victims in the offing.

When Berger and Weisman published their *Lancet* letter in 1997, it drew some predictable criticism. Squirrels have never been found to carry CJD, some people pointed out. Besides, they eat only fruit and nuts, not each other's brains. According to Weisman, however, city squirrel's "go after beef by-products all the time—like the suet that people put out for bids." Given CJD's long incubation period, Weisman told the *Times*, "there may have been an epidemic 30 years ago in the squirrel population."

There was only one way to test the hypothesis: capture some squirrels and check them for the disease. But even as state wildlife biologists were setting out traps, the squirrel-brain story was running wild—much to the state's dismay. It wasn't so much the threat of mad squirrel disease that rattled Kentuckians as the hillbilly portraits it inspired. Some admitted to eating brains, but few could remember presenting a squirrel head to the family matriarch, as Weisman told the *Times*, and fewer still remembered scraping squirrels off the highway for dinner. "Is there anything as gullible as a Yankee?" columnist Keith Lawrence wrote in the *Oswensboro Messenger-Inquirier*. "Somebody start printing up the bumper stickers now. 'I brake for squirrels. Mmmm-

mmmm good.'" *The Kentucky Post*, meanwhile, berated the eastern media for its "snobbish perception that the Bluegrass State is filled with shoeless, toothless, inbred, mouth-breathing, road-kill-eating hijacks so primitive as to chow down on anything that walks, crawls, or slithers." It wasn't long before Weisman's referrals were drying up, and the father of a hockey player he coached was taunting him during practice.

Sitting in his sunroom, recalling the controversy, Weisman hunches his shoulders and his features darken behind his glasses and beard. He doesn't like to talk about it, he says—this is the first interview he's granted since the story came out. But the words stream out anyway in a low, embittered monotone. He alludes to anti-Semitism and says his colleagues abandoned him. He calls parts of western Kentucky "strongholds of white supremacy" and asks if Rector is a member of the Klan. He insists that the *Times* misquoted him, that he never said Kentuckians eat roadkill.

"How could they say I don't know anything about local culture?" he says, "My own stepdaughter was the first International Barbecue Festival Queen! I watched her put on her costume and makeup in this house before the parade." He jabs a cigarette at a framed picture of a young woman on the wall. Then he leaps up and leads me to the foot of the staircase. "Look at this," he says, pointing to a stuffed red squirrel, slightly flea-bitten, standing there like a supplicant. "My wife bought that for me for my birthday." Then he adds offhandedly, "She grew up eating squirrel brains, you know."

Across the room, his wife, Beverly, sits primly on the sofa, as if patiently awaiting this revelation. When I arrived she was wearing a T-shirt and jeans, but while Eric was talking, she disappeared into the bedroom for a makeover. She has on green silk pants now and a purple batik blouse. He hair is pulled back in an elegant knot, and rouge and fresh mascara highlight her beauty-queen cheekbones, her kind, slightly asymmetrical eyes. "It's true," she says with a half smile. "I used to go squirrel hunting with my dad when I was a little kid. The brains were kind of a delicacy." She hasn't eaten them in thirty years, she adds, and she doesn't quite believe they can cause disease. But she helped Eric with his research anyway. When the letter was published in the *Lancet*, she was listed as a coauthor.

They make an odd pair, sitting on opposite sides of the room: New England intellectual and Kentucky farmgirl, gentile and Jew, yoked together by their dissatisfactions. When they met at the regional medical center, Weisman was already eager for his next move; she was an intensive care nurse, dreaming of medical school and the wider world beyond it. But instead of leaving Kentucky, he opened the Neurobehavioral Institute. "The circumstances kind of set me up," he says. "I had to show people that I could set down roots." And when Eric needed help, Beverly joined him as nurse, bookkeeper, and receptionist—deferring medical school indefinitely.

Every morning now he reads the *Boston Globe* and the *Boston Herald* on-line. Every night he watches the Red Sox on TV, noting the scores on sheets of paper taped to the refrigerator door. (Beverly had become a fan, too, he says.) He plays drums in his music room, travels to conferences, and keeps Kentucky at arm's length. "If I didn't have cable TV and a computer, I probably would have moved by now," he says. "But this way, it's almost like I'm living in Boston. It's just easier to find a parking spot." I ask him if he ever feels isolated. No, he says, pointing his thumb across the river to Ohio. "There's the North right there."

—

The day's kill has been skinned and gutted by now, washed clean of blood clots and flies, and soaked in saltwater for a few hours. Standing at his kitchen sink, Steve Rector pats the pieces dry and salts them generously as his basset hounds, Buford and Macie, look on. They get to eat the tails but not the meat, he says, rubbing Macie's belly with his foot—"She's so fat, there's enough room in there to fit another dog." But hope springs eternal.

We killed two gray squirrels and one red squirrel this morning, though two of their heads were too shot up to keep. The limbs, glistening against the porcelain, could be mistaken for rabbit or dove, but never chicken: the bones are too delicate, the flesh to dark and tightly muscled. Rector coats them in self-rising flour, then fries them in an electric skillet filled with hot oil. When the squirrel is nicely browned on both sides, he moves the pieces to a pressure cooker. "This is the healthiest meal there is," he says, throwing a few handfuls of flour into the bubbling oil. "It hardly has any fat or cholesterol at all." Then he adds more salt, shakes in a substance called Kitchen Bouquet ("That's just to turn it brown"), and pours the gravy into the pressure cooker with the meat. Once the top starts jiggling, he says, it'll be done in fifteen minutes.

Standing there, girding myself for the coming meal, I try to imagine myself as John Lawson, an early American explorer whose diaries I've been reading. In 1700, when Indian guides led Lawson through the Carolina wilderness, he happily feasted on raccoon, opossum, and bear fat. Beaver is "sweet Food," he declared, "especially their Tail," and skunk meat "has no manner of ill Smell, when the Bladder is out." Among the Indians, Lawson noted, a meal in great demand consisted of "two young Fawns, taken out of the Doe's Bellies, and boil'd in the same slimy Bags Nature had plac'd them in, and one of the Country-Hares, stew'd with the Guts in her Belly, and her Skin with the Hair on."

Squirrel meat is one of the last holdovers from

those older, immeasurably wilder days. Until 1996 even *Joy of Cooking* had some recipes for it, complete with a drawing of a boot standing on a squirrel's hide and a hand reaching down to yank out the meat. Now mad-cow disease and other epidemics, real and imagined, are chasing the wild game from our diet and once and for all. "I can serve Chilean sea bass any day," one Southern chef told me. "But if I serve large-mouth bass from a local lake, the health department could shut me down." In fact, no restaurants in the country can serve game legally unless it's raised on a farm, and fewer and fewer people prepare it at home. In 1997, when *Joy of Cooking* was overhauled, the squirrel section was quietly deleted.

"I watched my grandmother eat squirrel, and my mother eat squirrel, and I eat squirrel," Rector says. "But my son, he won't touch it. 'Daddy,' he says, 'that looks too much like a rat to me.'" His son is a deer hunter now, like everyone else around here. "There was a time, back in the sixties, when Kentucky didn't have any deer, and you could hunt squirrel just about anywhere." Rector says. But the coal company stripped everything out that squirrels would eat— sixty thousand acres of black oak and black walnut, mulberry, dogwood, and hickory. The first thing that grew back was honeysuckle and saw brier: perfect browse for deer.

When Steve Rector and Jimmy Vincent were kids, it seemed as if the land had no limits, and its rhythms were the only clock they followed. They'd drive anywhere they wanted, split up for a few hours, and meet back at the truck when the katydids hollered. But when the deer came in, local farmers got smart. "First they started charging a dollar an acre for lettin' me hunt. Then the next year it was two, then three, then eight. Pretty soon, the deer hunters were kickin' me off the land, when I was just tryin' to shoot squirrels." Nowadays, Steve has only four places left to hunt—one of them next to the power plant where he works. "I'm a dinosaur," he says. "Nobody hunts squirrel anymore." But he still manages to put a hundred squirrels in the freezer every fall.

It's been six hours since we last ate, I'm reminded, and for the past half hour we've been enveloped by the smell of frying meat. Perhaps that explains why I'm suddenly more open to the thought of consuming rodent. "I was watchin' the Discovery Channel the other day, and it was sayin' rat is a delicacy in some places," Rector says, emptying his pressure cooker on to a plate. "It's just a different concept. It's like we look at a cow and think that's somethin' you eat, and we look at a horse and say that's somethin' you ride. But a horse probably tastes even better than a cow."

I hesitate for a second, staring at the creamy mass of jumbled limbs. But when I take my first bite, the meat is tender and its taste straightforward—sweeter and richer than rabbit, I think, although it's hard to tell through the Kitchen Bouquet. By the time Rector reaches for the only head, I almost envy him.

"Here's how you eat one of these," he says, lifting up the skull with his fingertips. Seen in profile, it looks like the head of a monstrous ant: streamlined and mechanical, with buck teeth in front and incisors curving down the sides like whiskers. First Rector nibbles off the neck meat, then the cheeks, then he pulls off the lower jaw and plucks out the grayish-blue tongue. When all that's left is the braincase, he picks up a teaspoon and smacks it down smartly on top.

Inside, beneath the eggshell-thin surface, lies a pink organ about as large as the first joint of my thumb, stained inky black between its lobes. If some infectious agent lurks there, no pressure cooker could have killed it: brain tissue from a mad cow can pass on the disease even after baking in a seven-hundred-degree oven. "Ya want some?" Rector asks, holding the glistening brain toward me. Before I can answer, he pops it into his mouth. "Too late," he says.

—

Late one morning, after another few hours of hunting, I head for Louisville and Lexington, leaving western Kentucky behind. The clock jumps forward an hour as I drive east, but a small town gives way to cityscape, it feels like a millennium or two have passed. Along the highway, at first, there seem to be more pedestrians than drivers: broken-down old men waving flags around concrete barriers; women with bad backs and distended bellies, holding up signs that say "SLOW." But the construction clears eventually, and the faces give way to gleaming headlights, hurtling headlong for modernity.

"Let me give you a sense of the culture shock," Joseph Berger tells me later, reclining in his office high above the campus in Lexington. "When we first moved here from Miami, my wife went to our little grocery store one time and asked the proprietor if he had any Danishes. 'Ma'am,' he told her, 'we don't have Finnish, we don't have Swedish, we don't have Norwegian, and we certainly don't have Danish. But if you'd like a Twinkie, it's over there.'" Berger points toward an imaginary counter and bursts into an infectious giggle, his small round face and dark brown eyes turning even more impish than usual.

Berger grew up outside of Harrisburg, Pennsylvania, and has spent most of his adult life on the East Coast. He attended medical school in Philadelphia and for fourteen years was a professor of neurology at the University of Miami in Florida. When he got the offer from Kentucky, he says, he first had to find it on a map, but the chairmanship of a department was too much to turn down. Sure, it took a while to get used to the place. "When we first moved here, I was having my bread baked and half-frozen and brought in from Chicago. My meat was all imported, and I had those French cookies that I particularly liked—Petit Beurres—shipped in from friends in France." But there's been a sea change in the past four and a half years, he says, a "tremendous maturation" in the city: "There's no fine French restaurant yet, but we do have some decent nouvelle cuisine, as well as Mexican and Japanese restaurants." A few stores have been started carrying Petit Beurres.

The squirrel-brain letter was just an accident of circumstance, it seems, a spin-off from an old interest colliding with new surroundings. Berger had seen more than twenty cases of CJD in Florida—a surprising number, given its rarity—and became the medical director of the Creutzfeldt-Jakob Foundation, but he'd never known so many to have so odd a common trait. "In putting this letter together for the *Lancet*, I did it almost tongue-in-cheek," he says. "Had I known how prevalent squirrel consumption was, and how volatile the issue would be, I probably wouldn't have bothered to report it."

Berger's ambivalence is understandable, if a bit convenient. Since his and Weisman's letter was published, only one other squirrel-brain eater in Kentucky has been found to carry CJD. In 1998, the state Department of Fish and Wildlife killed almost fifty squirrels in western Kentucky, but by then fears of CJD infection in the state were so widespread that lab technicians refused to autopsy them. Frank Bastian, the CJD expert in Alabama, eventually agreed to examine the Kentucky squirrels at his lab. But he found no evidence of disease in their brains: no spongelike holes, no profusion of glial cells, no signs of any infection at all.

Fifty squirrels are hardly a representative sample, Weisman points out. "Even if you are looking at the right squirrels, you might still miss it. What are you supposed to look for? No one has even seen mad-squirrel disease before." Bastian agrees. Until he searches the brains for prions and spiroplasma, he says, the negative autopsies "don't mean anything at all."

But when I quoted Bastian to Ermias Belay, the epidemiologist in charge of CJD studies at the Centers for Disease Control in Atlanta, he let out a long, low chuckle. "Well, it means something to me," he said, then chuckled some more. After the *Lancet* letter appeared, Belay called the Kentucky Department of Health to check the state's CJD rate. "It wasn't a hell of a lot different from other states'," he says. "That doesn't rule it out, but you would expect it to be higher." Next he called a squirrel expert, who told him that squirrels live less than five years on average, making them poor candidates for a slow-incubating disease like CJD. Finally he took a closer look at Berger's and Weisman's material.

Cause and coincidence are hard enough to tease apart for most disease clusters, Belay says. But for CJD it's almost impossible. "What does it matter if you have two cases in the same neighborhood, when you know that they probably contracted the disease twenty or thirty years ago, when they lived in different states?" The *Lancet* letter blundered blithely into such statistical pitfalls. Berger and Weisman hardly examined the countless other common traits that surely connected their five CJD patients. Squirrel-brain eating seemed so exotic, so reminiscent of what caused mad-cow disease, that they felt compelled to single it out. Yet if their surveys were representative, more than a million Kentuckians have eaten squirrel brains at some point in their lives. Fewer than that, Belay points, have green eyes. "If those same CJD cases all had green eyes, would you then say that green eyes are associated with CJD?"

Weisman remains unswayed by such arguments. "All I know is everyone with CJD that I saw ate squirrels," he says, "and not that many people eat squirrels and not that many people have CJD." But Berger has long since parted company with him. The risk of getting CJD from squirrel brains is "vanishingly small," he now says. If a squirrel brain were offered him, he would probably decline it. "But if you feel funny refusing it go ahead and eat the damn thing."

As for Belay, he is less concerned about CJD from squirrels than CJD from deer (though even that doesn't worry him much). In southeastern Wyoming and north-central Colorado, deer and elk have been found to carry a form of the disease known as "chronic wasting disease," and many more Americans eat venison than squirrel brains. A few deer hunters have contracted CJD, and the *Times* ran a story on the topic similar to the one on squirrel brains, but Letterman and Leno never quite got around to working mad deer into their monologues. Chances are they'd eaten some venison lately. And deadly diseases are never quite as funny when you might get them yourself.

These days, the epidemic of epidemic stories seems to be dying down at last. Reporters have moved on to newer, fresher fears, and even mad-cow disease seems to be petering out: only ten new human victims were reported in Britain in 1999, and only 1,600 cows caught the disease—down from around 6,000 in 1997. The *Lancet*, for its part, is unlikely to publish a follow-up letter about squirrel brains, much less a retraction. "It's very hard, in science, to prove that something never existed," Belay says. "And when you do, people are not usually interested."

Kentuckians, in any case, have long since made up their own minds. Only a year after the controversy erupted, Rector gave a squirrel-cooking demonstration at the Kentucky's Folklife Festival in Frankfort. When he was done, he says, a local health inspector had to shoo people away to keep them from having a taste. "One elderly lady came up to me afterward," Rector remembers. " 'If I can't eat this squirrel,' she said, 'can I just take this biscuit and dip it in the gravy?'"

—

A year later, at the same festival, I wait under an open tent for Rector to give another demonstration—this time of guitar playing. Up and down the mall of the state capital, quilt makers, basket weavers, and wood whittlers are earnestly expounding their craft. Coal miners, on the "Narrative Stage," are telling stories from underground, while cooks, in the "Foodways Area," are stirring an enormous kettle of burgoo—a hearty stew that was long made with squirrel meat. The whole scene is both authentic and deeply contrived, edifying and dispiritingly predictable. But for a day, at least, it turns the tables on popular culture: tradition matters more here than the marketplace, and a good story has more authority than any scientific study.

When Rector shambles on stage of the day's last session, he hardly seems to notice that he tent is almost empty. Though the festival guides calls him "a key figure in the music of his region," Rector knows by now that his style is too eclectic for the average folk fan. Settling gingerly into small folding chair, like a walrus balancing on a rubber ball, he lays his acoustic guitar on his knee and silently fingers the fret board. He talks awhile about his teacher, Mose Rager, who invented the tumb-picking style, and about his idols, Merle Travis and Chet Atkins, who perfected it. Then he feathers a few harmonics to verify his tuning, plucks a chord or two, and he's off. "Bed-Bug Blues" at full throttle.

In the latter stages of mad-cow disease, patients may twitch so badly that they can barely hold a coffee cup. But Rector seems to be doing all right. Though his fingers are stubby and thick-knuckled, with nails so ragged that he has to wear paste-ons for concerts, they look as nimble as acrobats dancing on steel tightropes. While his thumb snaps the bass line and the heel of his hand thumps and dampens the soundboard, the other fingers play the melody and ornaments. They contort themselves into odd chord positions, then skitter down the strings for solos; they swing wide for bent notes, then hop up the fret board again side by side. During one particularly tortured run, a nail pops off and flies into the crowd. But Rector doesn't miss a lick.

For the next forty-five minutes his set follows an ascending curve of virtuosity. He plays a few more blues tunes for the traditionalists in the crowd, then gradually chucks in the rest of popular music: "The Shadow of Your Smile" and the theme from "Popeye," Duke Ellington, Elvis Presley, and John Philip Sousa, with his pinkie playing the piccolo part. Though his eyes stay glued to the fret board—out of shyness rather than necessity—a look of rising delight plays across his clenched features. "I haven't practiced this one in a while," he mumbles, and promptly seems to make a series of mistakes. Then I realize that he's really playing two songs at once: "Yankee Doodle" in the bass and "Dixie" in the treble—the perfect anthem for Kentucky, whose soldiers fought on both sides in the Civil War.

—

Watching Rector's fingers travel up the guitar neck, seeming to grow more confident the more difficult their position, I remember riding in this truck after our last hunt together. He'd shown me most of his childhood hangouts and hunting spots by then, but before I left he wanted me to see the Rochester Dam, the one John Prine sings about in the last stanza of "Paradise":

When I die, let my ashes float down the Green River
Let my soul roll on up to the Rochester Dam
I'll be halfway to heaven with Paradise waiting
Just five miles away from wherever I am.

Those words always reminded him of his cousin, he said. Jimmy never could get used to losing his old hunting grounds. Without a guitar or children to distract him, he couldn't stand to keep going to the same small patches of forest every week, where once he'd had the whole countryside, "You know that Indian?" he once told Rector. "The one in the pollution commercials that's always cryin'? I feel just like that Indian."

After his wife left him, Jimmy twice tried to kill himself, but both times he was too drunk to succeed. He used a long-barreled shotgun the first time and blew out part of his jaw. He aimed at his heart the next time and blasted off a piece of his shoulder. The third time he got it right.

One by one, Rector said, his heroes had died around him: Jimmy and Merle, Mose and Chicken-hawk Murphy. "Chet's had cancer four times," he said, "and the last time they took a tumor the size of a hot dog out of his brain." Now, as we drove within sight of the river, Rector admitted that he was worried for himself—and mad-squirrel disease had nothing to do with it. "My doctor tells me I've got the heart of an old man," he said, "and I've been passin' a lot of blood. They want me to get a colonoscopy, but I know how that works: You get all cut up, and then you still die."

We parked on the shore and looked out at the drought-stricken river, its sandstone ledges and muddy shallows, dark bluffs and sunken caverns exposed to the sun. And I thought about how rarely we face the true topography of our fears. Though death winds its way through every living moment—in the cars careening past us and the chemicals coursing through us, in the thickening of our arteries, the withering of our cells, and the uncertain courage of our hearts—we submerge its traces almost completely, letting our hopes and routines wash over its implacable shores. Each generation has more time to confront its mortality, and each generation concocts more outlandish threats—whether from Alar or aliens, fluoride, power lines, or mad squirrels—to distract itself from the confrontation, to preserve the delusion that death can still be defeated.

Rector said that he might not live through the year, and his pale, possessed features showed that he meant it. But then, too, I could tell he was still riding his luck, hoping that colon cancer was just another death threat he could escape through inattention. "You know, I never did understand that line about his soul rollin' up to the Rochester Dam," he said, pointing at the gray-green waterfall below us. "To do that, it would have to float *upstream*." Then he gunned the engine and turned his truck toward home.

The Mall of the Wild

Ken Holyoak's fish hatchery, frog farm, and wild hog preserve sits on a small gravel drive guarded by a very large fish. Eight feet long and six feet high, bristling with exotic fins and fluorescent purple-and-yellow scales, the fish looks like a cross between a bluegill and a beetle—a Volkswagen Beetle, that is, circa 1969—and hovers above passing cars as if scanning for minnows. Even Holyoak doesn't recognize its species. "I just asked this feller that goes to my church to make me a feesh," he says, "and that's what he come up with."

Such a fish might make a splash in any setting, but in Holyoak's part of the country it has the quality of a vision. On every side, Georgia's coastal plain stretches to the horizon in a weary ostinato, its peanut fields and forests repeating endlessly from the swamps of Florida to the hills of Alabama. Twisted

oaks and linear pines sit so far back from the highway
that the sky seems to engulf them, and the locals have
little interest in raising the skyline. Alapaha, the
closest town, has no visible sign of industry and only
one restaurant—one so secretive that I drove past it
three times without seeing it, though I was famished
at the time. But then there is Holyoak's fish: a thing
both of the landscape and monstrously out of place;
a blazing seraph, come to warn you of man's
indignities to nature. Or maybe just to sell you a few
hybrid bass.

One day, while researching the country's balloon-
ing aquaculture industry, I came upon a press release
from a group called the Future Frog Farmers of
America (FFFA). "Move Over Chickens!" it declared.
"Here Come the Bud Boys!" After thirty-five years
and a million dollars of investment, Ken Holyoak had
finally grasped the slipperiest of holy grails: a way to
mass-produce frogs. "Anyone who is remotely
familiar with bullfrogs realizes immediately that frogs
are discriminate feeders," the release said. But
Holyoak had taught his frogs to eat food that didn't
move, and he had a patented system for growing them
with little or no manual labor. Thanks to his techniques, frog farms might soon spread across the
country like the poultry industry. "Ken still has to
pinch himself to make sure he is not dreaming . . .
"No! He is not dreaming anymore! It is Bullfrog
Reality!"

This was news to me. I knew that frog gigging is an old southern tradition, and I'd grown up with kids who still caught their family dinner, on occasion, with a flashlight and a forked stick. But I also knew that frog legs have never quite made the leap into mainstream American cooking. As a chef I know put it: "A frog is either lowbrow or highbrow. If you catch it, it's low. If you order it in a French restaurant, it's high."

The FFFA promised to change all that. Frog demand, they insisted, is a function of frog supply. The United States imports 3,800 tons of frog meat a year—more than any other country—and schools take another two million live frogs, at $20 apiece, for class dissections. But with a good domestic supply, the FFFA believed, the total market might be worth more than a billion dollars. Add the profits from tanned frog skins, frog intestines as surgical supplies, and frog-oil cosmetics, and you had a gold mine in the making.

As novel as it seemed, the pitch had a familiar ring to it. I knew that aquaculture and game farms were changing the face of the southern landscape, and with them the economies of several states. But I also knew that such farms are a natural breeding ground for fraud. For every one hundred legitimate catfish or wild-game farms, there are two or three Ponzi schemes—breeding animals for a nonexistent market, making money only so long as there are new suckers to lure in.

On my way to Holyoak's hatchery, I stopped off to talk to Jeff Jackson, a professor of wildlife management at the University of Georgia. Over the years Jackson had made something of a hobby of busting quacks. He had exposed crooked worm farmers, kept a sharp eye on emu and ostrich suppliers, and pulled the rug out from under a beaver ranch. When I told him where I was going, his eyes lit up like Pat Garrett's at rumors of Billy the Kid. Holyoak was a special case, he said. He'd been selling fish for decades and had trademarked a popular hybrid sunfish called the Georgia Giant. "But when he talks about frog farms . . ." Jackson looked away wistfully. "I wish I could go with you and ask a few questions. But he'd be on to me right away."

—

Holyoak's office was a plain, cement-block structure with windows on four sides. Inside, stuffed bass floated along every wall, mounted on plaques inscribed by friends and happy customers. Holyoak, flanked by four local secretaries and ranks of untidy cabinets, spieled away on the phone, reclining so far that his chair back was nearly horizontal. As much as anything else here, his body was the product of selective breeding: 245 pounds of Georgia good ol' boy, hybridized from local and Utah Mormon stock, born and raised on the swamp. "I've got somethin' I got to show you," he murmured into the mouthpiece, his consonants muffled yet gravelly, like the sound of a country road heard from inside a car. "I've got to show it to you real bad." Along the walls, the fish rose toward their imaginary lures, mouths gaping, eyes mesmerized.

After brief introductions to his staff, I settled down to talk frog, but just then the door burst open. In walked a meaty, impatient little man dressed in a striped knit shirt. "My name is J. C. Bell," he said, "and I'm looking for some advice on fish." It seemed he owned an experimental farm about twenty-five miles away. Poultry, cattle, sheep, and goats grew there, all grazing the same pasture in strict rotation. Cows mowed the grass, then laying hens scratched through the cow patties for bugs. The scattered dung encouraged weeds, which the sheep and goats liked to eat, and pecan trees turned their dung into nuts. It was a three-hundred-acre farm, Bell concluded, making $1,000 profit an acre, and the products were all natural. "If I can just find a fish that'll eat the animal by-products, I can close the loop."

Holyoak nodded his head and peered at Bell for a long moment, from above his black reading glasses. "Try piranha," he said.

Like most of his jokes, this one had a kernel of sense. Two years ago Holyoak had spent a month on the Amazon, living on a raft with native fishermen, scouting for new ideas. "We spoke hand language mostly," he said. "But they knew what I wanted. Got up every mornin' at four o'clock, jumped in a dugout canoe, and went six miles down the river to fish in a dead lake. Monkeys and fish, that's all they ate. I took the fish." He lost fifty pounds, he added, but he developed an appreciation for piranha.

Bell was unconvinced. "I was hoping some catfish might do the trick," he said. But he agreed to come back with some water samples from his pond. "Maybe tilapia will work," Holyoak called out as Bell left, "or African catfish!"

In the lull that followed, I tried to steer the discussion back to frogs. Once again, though, we were interrupted—this time by a family of nineteenth-century farmers, or so they seemed. The women were in bonnets and gingham dresses, the patriarch in black slacks, black suspenders, and a white straw hat. Though they looked Amish to me, they soon revealed themselves to be Lubavitcher jews, returning home to Kentucky by minivan after a Florida vacation.

While the secretaries watched, fascinated, the old man shuffled forward with his cane, aimed his bony, bearded chin at Holyoak, and assessed him with squinting eyes. "Have you got any night crawlers?" he asked in a faintly eastern European accent.

Holyoak looked him in the eyes and smiled. "No," he said. "But I've got something even better." He reached under his chair and pulled out a Tupperware bin the size of two shoeboxes. Inside, corkscrewed through a thick bedding of oat bran, lay hundreds of centipede-like creatures, faintly venomous looking, with tan and gold stripes—another of Holyoak's Amazon discoveries. "I call 'em super wiggle worms," he said, reaching a hand into the bin. "They'll keep in here for a year; all you have to do is add a slice of potato every now and then." One of the centipedes clasped on to his forefinger with its two front legs, then writhed around to find purchase for the others. "They wiggle better than anything I've ever seen," Holyoak said. "People are goin' crazy over 'em. They're gonna replace the cricket. They're gonna replace the worm."

The patriarch stared at him, befuddled. He shifted from foot to foot. He glanced at his son. Nope, I thought, he isn't biting. The centipedes were just too strange and, at $68 for two thousand, too steep an investment.

Ten minutes later he walked out with a bin under his arm and a new fishing pole besides.

—

Around here, Holyoak is fond of saying, you can get up at sunup and shoot a hog, bag a frog, catch a fish, and trap a turtle by sundown. Sometimes it seems that what he's running is less a hatchery than an amusement park—one that grows larger and more bewildering with each new enterprise. When his fish business needed boosting, Holyoak stuffed his catalogs with snake guards, pond aerators, and "Bug-O-Matic" feeders. When a herd of wild hogs invaded his land, he started a hog-hunting business. (He keeps them fat by dumping fifty-five-gallon drums of peanut butter in the woods.) When turtles started eating too many of his fish, he invented a "solar turtle trap" and sold his catch to a supplier in Florida.

The result, unlikely as it sounds, is a kind of microcosm of America's increasingly privatized wilderness. Over the past twenty years, as annual sales of hunting licenses have dropped from seventeen million to fourteen million, operations like Holyoak's have rushed in to fill the vacuum. Catfish were once considered fit only for other bottom feeders; now U.S. farms grow more than half a billion pounds every year; crawfish gross $45 million annually in Louisiana alone; and other animals are making the same transition. Bison ranches, deer ranches, pigeon, alligator, and turtle farms have sprung up across the South, and their meat is being served in the finest restaurants. In Boston, at Savenor's market, kangaroo meat sells for $14.99 a pound, camel for $34.99, lion for $21.99, and zebra for $39.99. All of it is raised on game farms in the United States.

Biologists worry that game farms incubate diseases and can water down the gene pool for some species. But for other species, living on a game ranch may be the only way to avoid extinction. More Indian black bucks live on game ranches in Texas, with its vast grasslands, than in their native land, and bison have made a similar comeback across the country. In 1972 there were fewer than 30,000 bison nationwide, relegated to a few paltry preserves. By 1992 there were 110,000 bison, and by 1999 there were 300,000. "The more people eat buffalo," one rancher told me, "the more buffalo there will be."

Holyoak made a similar argument. "Silent Spring is now here for the bullfrog," one of his leaflets declared. "Pollution, destruction of habitat and over-harvesting" are decimating frog populations world-wide. Frog farms may be their only hope, Holyoak suggested, yet glancing around his office I still heard Jackson's words in my ears. What if all this bustle and earnest business was just an elaborate ruse—a setup like the fake bookie's office in *The Sting*? As soon as I left, I imagined, the secretaries would stand up, take off their glasses, stop typing nonsense, and collect their checks from Holyoak. The computers and file cabinets would get trundled off, the stuffed fish would come down from the walls, and Holyoak would drive off in search of another small town, another scam.

I was wrong, of course. Those ponds out back, stretching to the horizon in rectilinear formation, were no painted backdrop, and those were real people calling in their orders. Though his claims were probably inflated and some of his products a bit strange, one thing was certain: Holyoak knew fish.

The question was, did he know frogs?

—

"During the millennia that frogs and men have lived in the same world," John Steinbeck writes in Cannery Row, "a pattern of hunt and parry has developed. . . . The rules of the game require the frog to wait until the final flicker of a second, when the net is descending, when the lance is in the air, when the finger squeezes the trigger, then the frog jumps, plops into the water, swims to the bottom and waits until the man goes away."

Trying to get a grip on Holyoak's life feels a little bit like that. Most self-made men spend half their time composing their autobiographies, editing out the failures and eliding the equivocations until their lives sound as propulsive and single-minded as Horatio Alger stories. Not Holyoak. Ask him when he started his hatchery or where he found his super wiggle worms, and his answers will trail off into misty generalizations: "It's been years and years" or "I've been just about everywhere." At first you think he's being evasive, but little by little you realize he just doesn't remember. "I've got too much to do today," he says, "to worry about yesterday."

The beginning, at least, is clear. He was born, appropriately enough, in Enigma, Georgia, six miles from Alapaha. (When I asked where the name comes from, he glanced over as if embarrassed for me. "Enigma means puzzle," he explained.) His father was a Mormon missionary, sent to Georgia from Geronimo, Arizona. He had a genius for numbers and a "photogenic memory," Holyoak remembers. "I wish I had half the mind he had. He could quote the Bible word for word, and he could do numbers in his head faster than any calculator I've ever seen." By the time he died he had grown his farm to six hundred acres and developed special systems for raising hogs and cows. Unfortunately for him, his son's talents lay elsewhere.

"When I told him I wanted to grow nothin' but fish, he about died," Holyoak remembers. "'Bout had a heart attack right there." But he might have seen it coming. From the age of five Holyoak would stand by the door and bawl until someone let him hold a fishing rod. By the age of eight he was scratching out pools in his backyard and dropping in his live catch. By the time he was a teenager he was providing most of the protein for his family.

It wasn't just that Holyoak liked fish, it was that he had a psychic connection to them. "I just understand what they're doin'," he says. "I can walk out by a pond and tell you where they are." Even today, when he drives around his grounds, his eyes constantly scan his ponds' surfaces for signs of trouble. That one is too acidic, this one is overpopulated, that one is infected by bacteria and needs to be drained. "Some of these things," he says, "I don't hardly know why I know 'em."

At the University of Georgia he discovered a second skill: making money. While other students relied on their parents for their allowances, Holyoak operated three or four ventures from the house he rented. First he sold sandwiches to other students, eventually hiring twelve salesmen to run orders for him. Then he started a side business in hypnosis for students who wanted to quit smoking. "I would just talk to 'em and they'd go under. Had this fellow from New York show me how." When the air force drafted him after graduation, he still managed to make some spending money selling pictures of other airmen to their girlfriends. "You could drop me in the middle of a desert," Holyoak said, "and I guarantee I'll have a business started within an hour."

After that, the details start to get fuzzy. He went to work for U.S. Steel at some point and won an award for "100 percent sales performance," whatever that means. He built a sprawling ranch house of white brick with Greco-Roman columns in front, buried both parents, and somehow found time to visit thirty-three countries to look at frogs. There was a first wife in there somewhere, and the birth of his son Hugh, and then another marriage and another boy, Jason. But the exact sequence is known to no one—least of all Holyoak.

"Go ahead! Guess how old Jason is!" his second wife, Judye, asked him one day while Holyoak and I were eating lunch at her kitchen counter. Holyoak cut a thick wedge from a raw Vidalia onion and put it in his mouth.

"Twenty-seven?"

"Thirty-one! Ken! How about Hugh?"

"Thirty-five?"

"Thirty-six!"

She put her hands on her hips and shook her head. The two of them were about as different as could be, she said. Take the food we were eating: pulled pork and butter beans, stewed cabbage, cornbread, and tomatoes and rice. She wouldn't eat it for the world, but he wouldn't let her serve anything else. While she had branched out into Victoriana and interior decorating, pant suits and fancy pastas, he was still doing the same things he'd always done and tuning out the world around him. "I'll bet you he doesn't even remember when we were married or how old I am," she said. "The only reason he knows my birthday is because it's a holiday."

Holyoak looked up, a gleam of genuine hope in his eyes. "Christmas?"

Judye stared hard at him for a moment, then smiled despite herself. "You can't believe anything he tells you," she said. "He's teasin' all the time." Holyoak jabbed his thumb in my direction and told her, "He doesn't know when I'm teasin' and when I'm tellin' the truth."

Only this much is certain: at some point Holyoak managed to bring his two gifts together. He started out small, growing run-of-the-mill bluegills on his daddy's land. But he soon became impatient. "Here we had hybrid strawberries and dogs and cats and seed corn, but we were growing the same fish that Columbus had," he says. "It just didn't add up to me." And so, for the next ten years, he dedicated his life to breeding the world's biggest bream.

"I made him from scratch," Holyoak said. "Built ten or twelve ponds, brought in fish from all over, the biggest I could find, and bred 'em together." For ten years, he invested everything he made—around $10,000 a year—until he had ten or twelve hybrids. "I called the best one the Georgia Giant," he says. "He grows 300 percent faster and 300 percent bigger and bites 300 percent better."

It's easy to question Holyoak's claims. His numbers have a suspicious consistency—ten or twelve fish, ten or twelve ponds, 300, 300, 300 percent—and Jeff Jackson is quick to point out that Holyoak didn't really invent the Georgia Giant: large hybrid bream occur naturally. Then, too, some of Holyoak's stories are simply outlandish. He insists, for instance, that Cubans and Haitians buy most of his turtles for use in voodoo and fertility rituals: "The Haitians, they put the turtle on a pedestal and worship him, and when they're done, they chop off his head and drink his blood. The Cubans tie him to their stomach and dance around. When he urinates, it means they'll be fertile. . . . 'Course you can't do that with a snappin' turtle."

Still, Holyoak's success is indisputable. His operation

has grown from one pond on two hundred acres to seventy-nine ponds on fifteen hundred acres, and now hatches forty-four million fish eggs a year. Even when he's giving you the runaround, it's hard not to admire his work ethic. From four in the morning until eleven at night, with two late-night patrols thrown in, he inspects ponds and makes sales pitches, invents gadgets, shoots hogs, and breeds fish. "I just keep lookin' for ways to make 'em better and bigger and faster growing," he says.

Without hindsight to hinder you, the future is a realm of perfect possibility.

—

"Make your hand into a fist, or it might get bit," Kevin, one of the hatchery workers, told me. "Then reach around inside until you feel somethin' strange." We were standing knee-deep in one of Holyoak's artificial ponds, pulling up one of the buoys deployed along its shores. Attached to the buoy was a thick nylon rope; attached to the rope was an army surplus fuel drum, banged up and perforated with rust: the preferred nesting hole for Holyoak's channel catfish.

Inside the black mouth of the drum, my knuckles scraped tentatively against a rough, flaking surface. I'd done my share of hand grabbing by now, but this time we weren't after fish. Halfway down the side I felt it: soft and spongy, with loose, flowing tatters like boiled egg white. Slowly uncurling my fingers, I felt along the thing's edges and delicately peeled them loose from the wall. Then I reached under the quivering mass, pulled it free, and floated it to the water's surface. There, glistening like living amber in the midday sun, were some twenty-five thousand catfish eggs: Holyoak's next generation.

Just why I was doing this wasn't clear, but I suspected it was a diversionary tactic. Over the past couple of days Holyoak had been feeding me frog information at about the pace of a Bug-O-Matic— that is, just slowly and regularly enough to keep me famished. I now knew how long his bullfrogs take to grow to full size (180 days) and how much feed they consume in that time (a pound and a half—about a dollar's worth—per pound of meat). I knew that a seminar in frog raising costs $1,000, that a complete system costs around $25,000, and that such a system should be able to churn out twenty-five thousand pounds of frog legs every year at a wholesale price of $6 a pound. After some prodding I'd even been shown Holyoak's top-secret "North American Raniculture Research Center": a domed, corrugated hangar where the frogs are raised.

"We can't stay long," Holyoak said, half blocking the door. "Those frogs spook easy." But I squeezed through anyway. Inside, a heavy vegetal smell hung in the air and a watery silence reigned. The room was filled with rank upon rank of algae-covered tubs, each about the size of a large kitchen sink, stacked five high and fifteen deep. Every stack had a pipe above it that sent water cascading down to the tubs below, and every tub was covered in black mesh to keep the frogs from hopping away. Just a few months ago, Holyoak said, there were 150,000 croakers in here—nearly 250 per tub—but they'd been selling so fast lately, there were hardly any left. I looked in on a couple of the survivors: wide-eyed and mute, their bodies like pools of green-and-yellow wax, they listened like Zen adepts to the sound of water falling. "They won't eat for strangers," Holyoak said when I asked why they weren't touching their food. "It upsets them. I don't know if they'll even eat for a camera."

Who was buying these frogs? When would their products reach the market? How much "perfecting" did his system still need? Holyoak's answer had been to dump me off here to collect fish eggs. "It takes about three days of this job before the snakes get ya," he said, deadpan, as I climbed out of his pickup. "So we take all the New York journalists we can get."

Working my way along the shore, feeling pale and ridiculous in my swimming trunks (the others were wearing T-shirts and hip waders), I passed the time compiling a list in my head:

TEN SIGNS THAT KEN HOLYOAK IS PARANOID

1. He won't let me see the frog hatchery.
2. He won't let me talk to his frog biologist.
3. He won't let me see his top-secret super wiggle worm breeding laboratory.

4. He says he "can't remember" what kind of worm the super wiggle worm is, and he won't let me ask his worm biologist.
5. He suspects that the Chinese sold him sterile frogs.
6. His office is surveyed by videocameras.
7. His land is posted with signs that say "Warning: This Area Is Patrolled by Trained Attack Dogs."
8. Twice a night, between midnight and four, he drives around his grounds looking for fish thieves.
9. He says he can't offer me a room in his house because it's full. Yet his house is enormous and he has no guests.
10. He suggests I spend my nights in the motor home where his father died, deep in the countryside. "Just don't walk out at night. My trained attack dog will kill ya."

Still, I had to admit: Holyoak's paranoia was not entirely misplaced. According to the journal World Aquaculture, frog farming was a field so starved for good ideas that "successful frog farmers often guard their technology closely." Later in the same issue, a graph showed how little aquatic species had been improved by breeders over the past sixty years— especially compared to other species. Up at the top, shooting across the grid like a Patriot missile, were chickens: between 1940 and 1990 they nearly tripled the speed at which they grew. Just below them were cattle, rising in an equally vertiginous line; then came pigs, which merely doubled their productivity. Since the 1970s Norwegian salmon had begun their own rapid ascent. But frogs were still scurrying well below the page somewhere, with emu and ostrich to keep them company.

After all those years of running a hatchery, of designing bigger and better fish and schooling them from embryo to adulthood, Holyoak must have been tempted to think that nature was his to control. But a frog is not so easily broken. Nothing else seems so docile yet so hard to domesticate, so vulnerable—like an exposed organ, pulsing in the open air—yet so suicidally stubborn. As a result, most frogs eaten today are caught in the wild, largely in Bangladesh and Southeast Asia. They are gigged or caught in nets, gutted and stripped clean, and then shipped around the world frozen: a tasty, if inconsistent, variety of meat. In Brazil frogs are grown in outdoor vats. In China they're grown in concrete tanks with perforated floors. But those operations turn a profit by hiring cheap labor and catering to the frog's way of life, not by domesticating it.

"These things are just not very tough," says C. Greg Lutz, an associate specialist in aquaculture at Louisiana State University (LSU). "They're very aggressive, but also very fragile, and they tend to succumb to all sorts of bacterial infections. If you grow them inside, you've got to wash down their whole habitat with chlorinated water every day, give 'em a light dose of bleach every day, and even then you run into disease problems."

In 1981, when Lutz first came to LSU, he joined ranks with the country's one true frog-farming expert: Dudley "Bud" Culley. By then Culley had spent twenty-five years trying to perfect an indoor frog-raising system, but year after year his food and labor costs were higher than the costs of frog legs from Asia. According to Lutz, Culley's frogs were reluctant to eat processed food—a crucial step in bringing down costs—and even when they did reach marketable size, they tended to cannibalize one another. By the time Lutz arrived, Culley was ready to clean out his lab and retire. "I helped in the grand slaughter," Lutz remembers. "Then we had a big frog fry."

—

At the end of another long day, I climbed on the back of a truck and headed toward the main hatchery building, an open-ended hangar of steel and concrete. There the gelatinous masses of eggs we'd collected would be dropped into one of two hundred metal troughs, bathed in a steady current of water, and gently jostled by paddle wheels. (In the wild, fish continually fan their eggs with their tails to oxygenate them.) At any given moment there could be bream, bass, crappie, catfish, grass carp, trout, or even Japanese koi growing in there, all at different stages of development. In some troughs the eggs were still quiescent; in others you could see a coiled twitching within them; in still others the fry had broken free and were beating futilely against the current. Snub-nosed and jet black, their tails whipping back and forth, they looked like little hair follicles in search of a scalp—a wig on the run.

The light was slowly fading, and I was weary and sunburned and crusted in slime. But while the others took a break when we arrived, scratching the mud from their boots with sticks, I decided to give it one last try. Turning to one of the older hatchery workers, a former manager at a Winn-Dixie, I asked if he knew how many frogs Holyoak sold every year. "I don't have any idea," he said. "I've never worked with those things." He was about to go on when one of the others signaled for him to shush. Grinning strangely, he walked over to a wooden post beside me and pointed at the intercom hanging there. Up in its left-hand corner, a small red light was burning. "Somebody over there," he said, nodding toward the office, "is listenin' in on us."

We glanced at each other in silence. Each of us, I imagined, was doing the same thing: madly rewinding the last minute's conversation, scanning for any self-incriminating quotes. Finally one of the younger guys broke in. "There's the man you need to talk to," he said, pointing through the hangar door. Out in the parking lot, a tall, angular figure shambled past, shoulders hunched and hands in his pockets.

His name was John Joyce. He had a master's degree in aquaculture and divided his time between the hatchery and the University of Georgia, where he was a research technician. He had short gray hair, protruding ears, and eyes that peered at you intensely for a moment, only to skitter off when you tried to meet them. He'd been with Holyoak off and on for twenty years, he said, mostly breeding fish and tending to their health troubles. But when I asked about the frogs, he started to fidget like a subpoenaed witness. "I don't know," he said. "They've had some problems lately."

For years, he explained, Holyoak simply collected frogs from his ponds and sold them to farmers a few dozen at a time. Then, five or six years before, he began to grow them in vats at the main hatchery building. "We fed 'em larvae and pellets at first," Joyce said. "After a couple of years we had a good breeding stock of frogs, eatin' just pellets."

It was a promising start. But though the frogs had learned to settle for fast food, their wild instincts were only napping: the minute Holyoak moved them to an open pond, they staged a mass escape.

"So that was two years down the drain," Joyce said. To make up for lost time, Holyoak flew to China to buy some domesticated breeders. But then the eggs they laid weren't fertile. In the end they had no choice but to collect thousands of bullfrogs from the wild again and to teach them to eat pellets.

Then the disease struck.

Holyoak's stacked trays were natural breeding grounds for bacteria, Joyce said, especially if the frogs were overcrowded. Once a frog got sick in one tray, his infection drained down to any neighbors beneath him. "Two summers ago, that building was full of frogs," he said. "But bacteria about wiped 'em out. They're down to less than twenty thousand now. And he hasn't sold that many of 'em."

Holyoak later denied this version of events, but Joyce had no reason to bad-mouth the operation— quite the opposite. Listening to him, I realized that Holyoak's frog farm hadn't cracked the amphibian code after all, but neither was it a Ponzi scheme. It was something altogether sadder and more grand: a failed dream. Holyoak had done his homework. His tray system showed Chinese and Brazilian influences; his indoor operation was similar to Culley's. Yet after thirty-five years of catching frogs and feeding them pellets, tinkering with automatic feeders and inventing vaccinators, the Future Frog Farmers of America were no closer to dropping their first name. "I've been watchin' him work on this thing for a long time, and he's never quite gotten it," Joyce said. "I don't know if he ever will."

—

Many days later, at the Horseradish Grill in Atlanta, I sat at a gleaming oak bar and awaited my dinner. Behind me, the sun-baked evening crowd lounged about in summer dresses and linen suits, under the heavy beams of the vaulted ceiling, as a fire blazed in the corner. "Let me suggest a Sancerre," the sommelier murmured as soft jazz wafted down from hidden speakers above him. "It's a great summer wine from the Loire valley, with a bit of a tang to stand up to what you'll be eating." Then he laughed despite himself and leaned in closer. "The truth is I have no idea what to suggest. About the only thing I've ever done with frogs is flatten 'em with a post."

Earlier that day I had dropped off a pair of bullfrog legs at the Grill's kitchen. I had been told, on good authority, that this was the finest authentic southern restaurant in the country and that the chef, David Berry, was a big fan of farm-raised game. When I had called to ask if he would prepare one of Holyoak's frogs for me, he had agreed immediately.

There was only one problem: The frog I brought wasn't raised by Holyoak.

Holyoak had promised to give me a frog before I left the hatchery, but when the time came, he said the North American Raniculture Research Center was locked. Instead he drove me out to a pond and pointed a high-powered rifle out the truck window. In the evening's whiskey-colored light, I could see a bull-frog's eyes floating on the surface like soap bubbles, mesmerized by passing clouds. Then suddenly he was cartwheeling across the water, belly flashing like a green-and-yellow whirligig, trailing a ragged red streamer as if in an excess of joy. "D'ya see how far that bullet blowed 'im?" Holyoak chuckled beside me. "I ain't got nothin' but hollow-points in here for shootin' hogs."

Now, as Berry set my dinner before me, it was hard to connect that memory with the thing on the plate. On the one hand, no meat is quite so recognizable— so luridly anatomical—as a pair of frog legs. Stripped of its slinky tights, each ligament, tendon, muscle, and articulated joint looked ready to leap across the room. But then the taste was worlds away from the swamp. Tender and buttery, with a subtle, amphibian chew, it was so mild that the Sancerre almost over-whelmed it. "I sautéed it for three or four minutes and then drizzled it with a lemon-caper sauce," Berry explained, settling in next to me. "Frog doesn't need a lot more than that."

I had thought that the moral of Holyoak's story was clear: Some things just aren't meant to be domesticated. But here, in the elegant finish of this dish, in its seamless transformation from bullet kill to haute cuisine, lay another story. All nature's stubbornness, I thought, is no match for a good imagination. We've taught pigs to find mushrooms and dogs to lead the blind, corn to manufacture its own pesticide and watermelons to grow without seeds. Why shouldn't the Holyoaks of the world one day domesticate anything on legs, turning frog farmers into princes of industry? For an ever more ravenous, ever more ingenious society, wild game is just another work in progress.

—

Not long after that meal I finally managed to track down Bud Culley, the grand old man of frog farming. He lives in Liberty, Mississippi, now, far from the scene of his final frog fry. But rather than stewing in bittersweet memories, he's already in the throes of a new venture. "We've got the only frogs we know in the world that are entirely on pelleted food!" he said over a crackling phone line. "They're on pellets from metamorphosis on up!" When I pressed him for details, though, he cut me short: "I make my living off this consulting, so I'm not going to give you a lot of information to spread around." Then he hung up.

Is he dreaming? you ask. Call it Bullfrog Reality.

Send in the Hounds

We will, fair queen, up to the mountain's top,
and mark the musical confusion of hounds and
echo in conjunction.
—*A Midsummer Night's Dream*, Act IV, scene i

A dark forest, far from any porch light or murmuring
highway. A gang of hard-bitten men, silent and
single-minded. A pack of howling dogs, circling rest-
lessly. These are things most women try to avoid.
Sondra Beck, though, has a curious habit of seeking
them out. "There ain't no natural reason to like it,"
she admits. "Stumbling out there in the night just to
listen to a dog howl—it doesn't make any sense." Yet
ever since the age of six, Beck has been a coon-
hunting fanatic. In the foothills of Oklahoma's
Kiamichi Mountains, where she has lived all her life,
the raccoons are in a constant state of alert: Beck

hunts them more than 340 nights a year.

Tonight was the first round of the Oklahoma State Professional Coon Hunters Kennel Club hunt in McAlester. Throughout the low-lying hills around us, "casts" of four dogs—one per coon hunter—were competing to see how many raccoons they could run up trees. (Raccoons are nocturnal, so they're always hunted at night.) A few minutes before, our judge had punched his stopwatch and the dogs had been released. Now, the first to strike a trail would win a hundred points, the second would get seventy-five, the third fifty, and the fourth twenty-five. The first dog to tree a coon would win a hundred points, the next one seventy-five, and so on. The dog who racked up the most points by the end of the night would win the cast.

Somewhere out there, in other words, a raccoon was running for its life, scrambling over branches and paddling across streams, trying to stay ahead of the gnashing teeth at its heels. As the dogs lost its scent and circled to rediscover it, their voices laced together and unraveled, climbing and falling through the stunted hardwood forest. I knew that coonhounds change voices as they hunt—bawling as they search, yelping when they strike a trail, and when the coon is finally treed, switching to a choppy bark that can carry for miles. But in that midnight dark their sounds were like radio signals from another galaxy. I heard a bark out there, a yip and a grunt or two, and what sounded like a ray gun. Then, abruptly, the noises faded, leaving us stranded in those strange woods.

"Which way did he go, George?"

"I can hear the blue bitch, but I think they're all lost."

"They'd get found if they'd come back this way."

With our headlamps off I could just make out five human shapes, their outlines faintly phosphorescent with starlight. Though I couldn't see their faces, I could imagine their expressions: a smirk here, a squint of concentration there, nowhere a hint of fear. Most of them knew this forest in the dark better than I knew my own neighborhood by day. Every passing scent belonged to a plant they could name and describe; every change in terrain fit the contours of some mental map. They knew where the wild persimmons and hackberries grew and whether they had ripened yet, and what they didn't know their dogs could tell them.

Beck's sinewy shape hunched over a cigarette ember, drawing in a long breath before exhaling. "I don't know what I'm doing with Sandy out here," she said. "She just had a litter seven weeks ago." Most hunters prefer larger, more aggressive males, but Beck has never had anything but females. "They may be in heat twice a year," she says, "but males are in it all year round." If she felt any sympathy for Sandy tonight, it was only because she had been in the same situation herself: two months after giving birth to her daughter, Beck was out in the woods again, hunting raccoons while her husband took care of the baby.

Suddenly a sharp, squeaky bark rifled through the woods, like the sound of an ax biting into hickory.

"Tree, K.C.!"

One by one the hounds' voices lifted from the same direction, sounding as hungry, if not quite as harmonious, as wolves. I waited for a long moment, but no one moved. "Can I turn on my headlamp now?" I whispered finally.

"Yeah," Beck said. "Go ahead."

But when the blinding light surrounded us again, I could understand her reluctance: in a forest at night, only those in the dark can truly see.

—

Beck's sixty-acre farm lies down a long dirt road in southeastern Oklahoma's Pushmataha County— "twenty miles from the nearest loaf a' bread," as she likes to say. The farm consists of a double-wide mobile home with a satellite dish, a dilapidated barn, two rectangular paddocks, and the Clear Creek Kennel, where she breeds perhaps the finest English coonhounds in the country. Pastureland lies all around and beyond it a circle of forest that drops, on one side, toward Clear Creek and some of the last virgin bottomland in Oklahoma.

For now it's still wild country—just driving to Beck's house, I passed snapping turtle, muskrat, skunk, armadillo, hawk, and raccoon lying along the roadside. But within a generation, she knows, much of the wilderness may be cut over as the last of the big landowners dies. (People here are sometimes poor and sometimes only posing as such: when one local farmer died not long ago, his relatives discovered that he owned fourteen blocks of downtown Oklahoma City.) "This is probably the last place around here like this," Beck says. "We can hunt for three days and nights without ever hitting the highway."

When I first came to Beck's farm, I'd recently become the proud but somewhat befuddled owner of a redbone coonhound—a dog bred, over the course of centuries, for the sole purpose of tracking and treeing raccoons. I knew that I would probably never hunt Hattie—I lived in Cambridge then—but I wanted to get a better sense of her heritage and what drove coon hunters into the woods night after night. The previous year, at another coon-hunting championship, Beck had been pointed out to me in the crowd. "That's our champion from the last two years," Bill Cavner, the secretary-treasurer of the Oklahoma Federation of Coon Hunters, told me. "Most of these guys are scared to death they'll draw her cast tonight." Afterward I'd called Beck a few times to talk about coon hunting, but this was my first time meeting her in the flesh.

Ambling out to greet me, she seemed to blend into the landscape as well as any coyote. At fifty-three

Beck was tall and rangy, with bristly, sandy blond hair, stone gray eyes, and weathered skin. Her voice was as hoarse and raucous as a raven's, but with a sweetness that kept it from being intimidating. Around those parts, I'd heard, Beck was famous for taking in strays—not just cats and dogs, but deer, goats, and pigs, too. "The game warden brings by any wild animals or orphans he finds, even though keeping them is illegal," she told me later, in her kitchen.

While I watched, she poured warm milk into two nipple-topped baby bottles and brought them out to her two orphan calves, Midnight and Curly Sue. In the neighboring paddock, a bunch of goats clanked around among the lawn detritus, their eyes maniacal above their bony bodies, while a pony and a pot-bellied pig named Louise looked on. "Over at McAlester prison, they train some mean dogs to walk between the fences, to prevent escapes," Beck said. "I have a friend who works over there who brought me a dog once that was just too mean for them. Well, I kept it chained up in our barn and fed it from a stick for a week. In the end that dog loved me. Always made my husband, Brent, nervous, but it would have done anything for me."

Some people might see a contradiction between caring for orphaned animals and chasing raccoons around every night. My mother, for instance, finds raccoons every bit as exotic and adorable as koalas. A native of Germany, she calls them "bears that wash themselves" and tends to sigh at their mention. When she and my father drove me to my first coon hunt, she suddenly turned and pleaded: "You aren't going to shoot any yourself, are you?" Later, when we passed a simple church entitled House of Prayer, my father looked over and grunted: "That's where you'll find all the raccoons right about now."

When I mentioned these qualms to Beck, she just shrugged: "This is bad country for animal rights activists." Back in the 1970s, when coon hides sold for $30 or $40 apiece, Beck used to earn her Christmas money coon hunting. (Winter, when raccoon pelts are thickest, is official coon-hunting season.) Some of her poorer neighbors went further, all but making their living from hides. "You couldn't really blame them," Beck said. "A man could work all week for $100, but he could make as much in two hours in the woods." Still, today, with raccoon coats out of fashion, pelts bring as little as seventy-five cents and most hunters have put away their guns, leaving only sportsmen behind. While the number of commercial coon hunters has plummeted, the number of coonhound events has nearly doubled in the past ten years. These days, at Christmastime, Beck puts out feeders for the raccoons rather than selling their hides.

This was a tale to gladden my mother's heart. But wildlife biologists, I later learned, are less than pleased by it. Raccoons and coonhounds, it seems, have spent most of American history locked in furious evolutionary competition, an arms race of sorts to see which side can outwit or outsmell the other. Like the cold war, the battle hasn't always been good for its participants, but it's been good for the world at large, giving the dogs something to chase and keeping the raccoons from eating everything in sight. Only lately, when coon hunters have declared détente, has all hell broken loose.

—

The story began some five centuries ago, when the first boatload of Spaniards arrived on the shores of the New World. American dogs were a motley crew back then. From the long-haired pueblo to the Mexican hairless to the Peruvian pug-nosed, there were seventeen types in total, all of them descended from wolves, coyotes, dingoes, and the Siberian dogs that followed the first Asian trekkers across the Bering Strait. "Surly and snappish . . . snarlish and intractable," in the words of one settler, they were used by native people to stampede bison over cliffs, to herd llama and alpaca, and to find the breathing holes of seals. But no historical account, no early Indian account, recalls dogs hunting down raccoons—much less chasing them up trees and barking like maniacs.

Then came the Spanish and their dogs of war. "They have eyes which shoot out fire, throw out sparks," wrote a Franciscan friar named Fray Bernardino Sahagún. "They are very stout and strong;

they are not peaceful, they go panting, they go with
their tongues hanging out. They are marked the
color of tigers, with many colored spots." In 1495
Christopher Columbus's twenty hounds ripped
through ranks of Indian warriors at the battle of
Vega Real in Hispaniola, a spectacle so terrifying
that many tribes later surrendered without a
fight. "Within a few years," anthropologist Marion
Schwartz writes in *A History of Dogs in the Early
Americas*, "public markets sold human body parts for
training Spanish dogs to develop a taste for people,
and these dogs were pitted against Native Americans
for sport."

Once the Indians got over the shock of facing such
animals, Schwartz goes on to say, "they were eager to
get their hands on this new 'technology.'" Soon
European dogs were interbreeding with local mutts,
adapting effortlessly to climates from the arctic to the
tropical, bearing offspring that would almost completely replace the native varieties. Just as the
Spanish brought their dogs of war, the French,
English, and Germans brought their own breeds,
carefully tailored for other tasks. There were slender,
sharp-sighted whippets and greyhounds, so fleet they
could outrun a deer; dachshunds for digging out
badgers; Airedales so strong they could stand up to a
wolf. But the true triumphs of the breeders' art were
the scent hounds.

In August of 1785 seven such beasts arrived at

George Washington's home in Mount Vernon, a gift from his friend the marquis de Lafayette. Known as Grand Bleu de Gascogne hounds, they were first bred in 1360 by Gaston Phoebus, comte de Foix. The Grand Bleus' noses were said to be the keenest of any breed, and their voices, Washington noted in his diary, rang across the Virginia forest like the bells of Moscow. Yet even they still needed some fine-tuning. For centuries, blue Gascon hounds had mostly hunted things that stayed on the ground: wolf, hare, deer, red fox, wild boar. Once in Virginia, however, they had to go after game with a penchant for heights: bobcats, American gray fox, mountain lions, raccoons. Dogs without a good treeing instinct were likely to charge right past their quarry or else abandon it before the owner caught up. Four months after receiving his French hounds, Washington complained that he was still "plagued with the Dogs running Hogs."

In time Washington would come to be called the father of coon hunting as well as the father of his country. But the truth is that creating coonhounds was a group effort. Content with any dog that exhibited the right instincts, other settlers threw English foxhounds, Cuban bloodhounds, Hanoverian schweisshunds, and red Irish hounds into the canine melting pot. By the 1800s new American breeds began to emerge, all with strong noses, floppy ears (for stirring up scents), insensitive coats (for tearing through brambles), and a peculiar passion for chasing things up trees. The United Kennel Club now registers six of them—English, Plott, bluetick, redbone, black and tan, and treeing Walker—but the elite American Kennel Club fully recognizes only black and tans. As one bluetick owner told me, "The AKC would rather register some strange, furry little animal in China than the dogs that helped build this country."

Sandy, the dog Beck would be hunting at the state competition, was the latest model in coonhound breeding and training. Trim and light on her feet—more foxhound than bloodhound—Sandy didn't waste time worrying out cold trails inch by inch, as a "cold-nosed" dog would. She skimmed over the terrain to home in on the freshest, "hottest" scent and ran it down as quickly as possible. Some hunters missed the behemoths they grew up with and the epic hunts those dogs used to lead, but Beck had no regrets. "In my opinion, the dogs have gotten better and better," she said. "Those old black and tans and blueticks, they might pick a trail three days old and howl and boo-hoo over it for hours and hours. I don't have any time for that. I need my dog to move that track."

—

Raccoons, meanwhile, have done some evolving of their own—thanks no less to European settlers. First hunters wiped out wolves, bears, mountain lions, and the raccoon's other natural enemies. Then settlers came in and created ideal raccoon habitats: successional forests grizzled with fruit bushes, villages free from predators, and cornfields laden with food. Finally, as a kind of bonus, we gave them garbage dumps to get them through the lean times. Two centuries ago no raccoon could get far from a forest or swamp without starving or being eaten. Now they're happily ensconced even in the prairie states.

Growing up in Oklahoma, reading *Where the Red Fern Grows*, I always thought of raccoons as underdogs. In that book a young boy kills enough of them, with the help of his two redbones, to lift his homesteading parents out of poverty. True, much is made of raccoons' wiles: Doubling back on their own tracks, swimming down rivers to erase their trails, leaping from treetop to treetop, they constantly pit their wits against overwhelming odds— small, furry Steve McQueens hoping for a Great Escape. But their struggle is clearly doomed: inevitably the dogs chase them up a tree and the kid shoots them down.

It was only later that I began to hear the other side of the story, the one where the raccoons got away. In the early 1940s, for instance, hunters in north-central Arkansas had a hard time treeing any coons at all for a while. The reason, they found, was a conveyor belt, built to carry rocks from a quarry to the nearby Bull Shoals dam. "Coons learned they could

get on that conveyor belt to get away from the dogs,"
Forrest Wood, a resident of nearby Flippin, Arkansas,
told a reporter. The tactic, he added, nearly drove
local hounds crazy. "Several dogs had to be locked up.
They just couldn't stand it."

So it went: raccoons ever scrambling into new
environmental niches; coonhounds ever evolving to
flush them out. For two centuries the race was a
dead heat, with raccoons expanding their range yet
supplying skins for countless coats and hats. Then,
in the 1980s, when raccoons became too worthless
to kill, the balance of power abruptly, disastrously,
shifted. With the last of their predators gone,
raccoon populations began to swell drastically.

Ecologist Justin Congdon remembers the change
more vividly than most. For the past twenty-five years
Congdon has followed the nesting habits of turtles
living in a single 1,500-acre preserve in southeastern
Michigan. Raccoons always ate their share of turtle
eggs, Congdon says, but the turtles were prolific
enough to cope: from 1976 to 1980, 40 percent of the
nests survived. Once fur prices plummeted, though,
raccoon populations reached "plague proportions":
for most of the 1980s only 4 percent of the nests
survived. "Some years," Congdon says, "out of 150
nests, 150 were destroyed." On Florida's Canaveral
Peninsula, in the same period, a study found that 397
out of 400 loggerhead sea turtles' nests had been
destroyed. More recently, in northern Louisiana,

raccoons have destroyed nearly all the turtle nests in a number of study sites.

Like most animal researchers, Congdon has a grudging respect for raccoons. Over the years lab studies have demonstrated the animal's intelligence—"Discrimination of the Number Three by a Raccoon," a typical paper is titled—and field studies have confirmed it. "They work an area just the way I do," Congdon says, "except they're not doing it for science, they're doing it for dinner." First the coons case the most popular nesting spots—road banks, fire lanes, dams. Then, when egg-laying season is at its peak, they converge. "I've seen a raccoon take the eggs from a female snapping turtle as they're being laid," Congdon says. "He just stood behind her, where she couldn't bite him, and caught the eggs in his hands." If the turtle is small enough—like a painted turtle—the raccoon will just bite its head off, eviscerate it from the esophagus down, and pluck the eggs from its oviduct.

The same sorts of stories are told by people who study neotropical birds and wild turkeys, whose eggs are also eaten by raccoons. Right now, they say, only diseases like rabies, distemper, and parvovirus are keeping coon populations in check. (After an epidemic, young raccoons sometimes have to learn to find their prey's nests again, since their mothers weren't around to teach them.) But the violent booms and busts are hard on a habitat. Much better, everyone agrees, would be to control the raccoons more consistently—for example, by hunting them. As one wildlife manager put it: "I wish the coon hunters would just go ahead and kill them."

—

Walking around the parking lot in McAlester, on the evening of the coon hunt, felt a bit like visiting an American military base: all that sleek, high-tech weaponry for what amounted to war games. Though the hunters looked as ragged as sharecroppers, few of them had spent less than $10,000 on coon hunting. Their hounds, though tied to tailgates with frayed lengths of rope, could fetch up to $20,000 from a breeder. Their beat-up trucks were crammed with electronic gear: radio-tracking systems, lamps with interchangeable lenses, and collars that could shock a dog's vocal cords if it barked up the wrong tree. When these men weren't demonstrating such gizmos, they were usually discussing their dogs' sperm count. Many of them regularly sent their champion studs to places like Galaxy Genetics Reproductive Center in Ohio. There, employees collect semen in a plastic vagina, package it in "straws" chilled by liquid nitrogen, and send it off by courier for next-day insemination.

Beck, as usual, was the only woman in hunting gear. "Some women, they try to love coon hunting 'cause that's what their husbands do," she said. But a coon hunter is born, not made. "I was a tomboy, of course. Now I'm an old woman and I'm still a tomboy," she said. "Now, my sister, she was different. She was all, you know, feminine and things. She was the type, you'd say 'spider' and she'd run a mile."

Another female coon hunter I'd spoken with, Vickie Lamb Deal from southern Georgia, had complained that it took her years to get the other hunters' respect. They held barbed-wire fences open for her, stuffed phone numbers in her pocket, and their wives grew so jealous that they sent her an anonymous letter. "They told me that I had no business hunting with men, that I should form my own club with other women," Deal said. "If they had just stopped to think about it, they would have realized that out in the swamp—with the mud and the bugs and the snakes—is not a particularly good place to flirt with someone's husband."

Beck hadn't had that kind of trouble. "I really don't think that they think of me as a woman hunter out there," she said. "There's no holding the fence for me, and that's the way I like it. If you put yourself in a man's place, you ought to be able to carry your weight." By now she'd hunted for so long and in so many places that everyone in the coon-hunting world knew her by name. But even when she drew a cast full of strangers, she never had a problem. "'Course, I never encourage nothin'," she said. "But I just think coon hunters are awful nice people. At least they are to me."

—

Three hours later, as we drove toward our third hunting site of the night, I could only envy her insouciance. As the roads grew thinner and more twisted, branches squeaked and scraped against the outside of the windows, and I could see our driver's face glistening with tension as he worked the wheel. "I don't whip my dogs much," he said, "but when I do I keep it up until they've got blood on their backs. That way they know they've been whipped."

We were having a tough night. A couple of hours before, we had hoped to surprise a few raccoons munching on ripe mulberries, but the dogs led us to huge, crooked post oaks instead. We probed the trees' branches with the beams of our headlamps and blasted on whistles designed to sound like an injured animal—raccoons are incurable rubberneckers—but our lamplights caught no glimmering, inquisitive eyes. For a while one of the hunters swore that he could see a dark shape in the upper branches, but the others ignored him. "He didn't see no coon," Beck muttered. "When another guy's light shines up on the other side of the tree, it can fool you sometimes. But it ain't a coon until three people see it."

Now there was less than half an hour left on the judge's stopwatch and we still hadn't seen any raccoons. Slogging through a marshy meadow ahead of me, the dogs and their owners looked equally abashed, their shapes stooped and spectral in the light of my headlamp. "Well, Katie, I don't know what the hell you're doin'," one hunter told his bluetick. "But it's about time you treed a damn coon."

Beck grinned next to me. She didn't usually talk to her dogs much on a hunt, she said. "But I like 'em to talk to me a little bit more than Sandy's been doin'." At such moments hunters used to comfort themselves with tales of raccoon subterfuge—of animals running on fences or down gravel roads to hide their scent—but competitive hunts, with their quick-treeing dogs, have changed the character of coon legends. Hunters now talk about how tough coons can be in a fight, how they can whip almost any dog one on one. The week before, Beck had been at a hunt in Paris, Texas, where four dogs had chased a raccoon into a lake. While the raccoon was in its element, the dogs were clumsy in the water and had to content themselves with circling and barking. The coon bided its time. When it noticed that one of the females was tiring, it calmly crawled on the dog's head and drowned her.

The hunters found the other three dogs an hour later, still swimming around the raccoon.

Tonight, halfway back to the trucks, our dogs flared another trail. As the minutes ticked off on the judge's stopwatch, we listened to the dogs toiling in the eaves of the mulberry grove, their voices insistent, exaggerated, as if trying to convince themselves as well as their owners. Fireflies drifted above the marsh grasses, like torches carried by a distant search party.

Then a blaring squall erupted from far to our left, well away from the other dogs.

"Tree, Sandy!"

While the other dogs were wasting time on cold trails, Beck's dog seemed to have peeled off and found a coon on her own. If so, this was a "split tree" in coon hunter parlance: the crowning skill of a well-trained coonhound. But Beck was suspicious. Her dog Alf would bark 135 times a minute when he treed a raccoon. And though Sandy wasn't quite so loquacious usually—she averaged 80 or 90 barks a minute—tonight she was downright taciturn. We tried to follow the sound of her voice, but minutes went by without a bark. When Sandy started up again, her voice had a hesitant, faltering quality, like a child who knew that she was lying but couldn't seem to remember the truth.

"Please, y'all, don't judge her by tonight," Beck said, gripping the top strands of a barbed-wire fence and scissoring her legs across. Sandy wasn't the quickest dog in her kennel, but she was usually a "classy" tree dog: up on her hind legs, propped stiffly against the trunk, head thrown back as she barked. By the time we reached her, however, she was cowering against the base of the trunk with the rest of the dogs. She looked up at Beck, clearly disconcerted, her only consolation being that the other dogs didn't know what to make of the situation, either.

We strafed the branches with our headlamps, still

hoping for a glimpse of flashing eyes. Like Sandy before us, we whooped just once at the sight of scuttling forms, then realized our mistake. These creatures were too small, too indifferent to our lights and noise, to be raccoons. The fringe of folded white fur along their sides eventually gave them away: flying squirrels.

In a night of misdirection and disappearing coons, this was the forest's final practical joke. Few in the cast had ever seen a flying squirrel before, though they had thousands of hunting hours between them. "I know my dog didn't tree those things," Beck said. "They don't hardly touch the ground to leave a scent."

John Dennis, the lowest-scoring hunter among us, reached down to leash his bluetick. When he stood up he was holding something he'd found in the leaves: a dirty Coke bottle with a scroll of paper wound up inside. Given how the night had gone, he probably expected the message to read, "Nyah, nyah, nyah." Instead it just said, "Hi, Fred." Dennis wadded up the note—"My name isn't Fred," he said—and threw it into the blackberry bushes.

—

Later, as we headed back to our trucks, the dogs were still straining at their leashes, eyes rolling back in their heads, desperate for more. What do they get out of all this? I wondered. Their days were spent in a cage or in training (some owners took them running down country roads, tied to a pickup driving at a steady clip), their nights in a forest hunting for something they'd never kill. What kept them going?

The answer wasn't clear. But I thought a clue to it might lie in a lecture I'd heard a year before, at a meeting of the American Association for the Advancement of Science. Two animal behaviorists from Hampshire College in Massachusetts had compared the sounds dogs make to those made by wolves. Genetically, for all intents and purposes, dogs are wolves: they share all but 0.2 percent of their mitochondrial DNA (wolves and coyotes are twenty times as genetically distinct). Beyond their appearance, the sole thing separating them is behavior. Although wolf pups whine just as dog pups do, wolves eventually graduate to growls and howls, while dogs never get past barking. A dog's bark, the scientists had said, was midway between a whine and a growl—a confused, "ComeHereGoAway!" sound indicative of arrested adolescence.

Dependent, petulant, overly excitable, most dogs are easy to imagine as terminal teenagers. But these coonhounds were different: though loyal beyond reason, they had careers of their own, in a sense. I remembered going to buy Hattie at a breeder's house, expecting to be chased by a pack of bloodthirsty dogs as I came up the driveway. But they barely turned their heads at my arrival: "Go on," their eyes seemed to say. "You aren't what we're after." On this night, listening to the dogs howling down the trail, so nearly like a pack of wolves, I couldn't help but wonder if they hadn't managed, against all odds, to break free of their adolescence, to transcend their domesticity by returning to the hunt.

The more elusive question was what kept the owners out here. A competitive hunt was exciting, sure, but what about all those other nights, alone in the woods without a trophy to win? "It's a simple deduction," one coon hunter told me. "You love it or you hate it. And even if you hate it, you can't quit it. It's as bad as bein' a damn dope addict." No coon hunter really expects to make his investment back with breeding and prize money, Beck admitted. Yet pleasure wasn't really the point, either. "There are some nights, before I go on a hunt, when it's kind of cold outside and I'd rather stay home and watch TV," she said. "But I don't think of it like that. When it's dark, I just go hunting."

Both Beck and her husband, Brent, had been married before, and they seemed to keep a certain teasing distance from each other. Although they were often in the woods together, they always trained and hunted with their own dogs—Brent mostly with males, Beck always with females. During the week Brent worked full-time at an ammunition depot in McAlester, but he still managed to match Beck's training regimen. He'd take two young dogs with him on Monday, spend three nights training them after work, and then come home for the last four nights of the week.

"Yeah, I kind of believe there might be some competition there," Beck told me. "A lot of times, even when we're just pleasure hunting, we'll go by competition rules to practice." In 1991, Brent and Beck both advanced to the quarterfinals of the UKC world coon-hunting championships, only to draw each other in a cast. "They changed the rules after that so that two dogs from the same owners can't ever be in the same cast together," Beck said. "Why would you want to pay a $500 entrance fee just to be eliminated on the first night by your own dog?" As it turned out, she won the cast.

—

By the time we made it back to Beck's farm, the pastures were glowing grayly in the false dawn, and I would have been more than happy to sleep in the kennel. Moving at half speed, Beck led me to her mobile home, but she seemed reluctant to open the door. "We're a different breed out here," she said, glancing in at the flimsy gold paneling and faux wrought-iron latches, the worn shag carpeting and plywood cabinets. "Beyond civilization." She made up a pallet of quilts for me on the floor, in front of the console television, then sat on the arm of the couch, her face half in shadow. There was a house here once, she said, but it burned down because of a faulty hot-water heater, and they spent the insurance money on their trailer and kennels. "There're a lot of things I would change if I could."

Though Beck still lived in her hometown, and though she'd married twice and had five grand-children, her dogs were her true legacy. Her own children had only confirmed her belief that a love of coon hunting can't be taught. "I tried to get my kids interested," she said, "but it never did seem to stick. They're town kids by nature—town kids who just happened to be raised in the country. I remember one time, we took 'em out to the woods and my husband was shining a light on a coon to show my daughter, to get her interested. Well, I suddenly noticed my son was missing. I called around, but I couldn't find him, and I was starting to get real worried. When I finally found him, you know where he was? Sittin' in the grass, using a penlight to read a Hardy Boys novel." He is a computer programmer in Dallas now.

All around us, in the dingy light, trophies lined the walls in triple ranks, their golden figurines and silver hounds gathered in a great circle around me, like miniature gods awaiting a coon hunt on Mt. Olympus. Over the past ten years Beck and Brent had won the Oklahoma State Coon-hunting Champion-ship twice and the Oklahoma State Nite Champion hunt four times; they'd placed second in the Texas State Coon-hunting Championship and in the pres-tigious UKC American Heritage hunt, qualified more than fifteen dogs for the UKC World Championships (five in a single year), and won countless smaller hunts. Over in the corner, a gigantic, four-tiered purple trophy commemorated a hunt that their dog Cadillac had won in 1994, in what was then the largest open event in history. "I need to get rid of a bunch of those," Beck said, following my gaze. "I have boxes and boxes of plaques in storage."

Brent nodded on his way to the bedroom. "You can't eat trophies," he said. "You can boil 'em three days and the soup's still bad."

Beck and I sat quietly for a moment then, listening to the night sounds outside. And I wondered how it changes a person to know the sleeping world as well as the waking one. I got up each day to the relentless immediacy of the world at work—the clamor for attention, for conversation, for instant gratification. But Beck had spent half her waking life watching the world at rest. Driving home after a long hunt, she could probably picture her grandfather still alive within one of those darkened farmhouses, her husband a dreaming child, her children asleep with families of their own. In the half-light between dark night and morning it was easy to confuse the future and the past, the hills an empty stage for your imagining.

After a while Beck groaned to her feet and cast a last look around—a look that seemed to encompass all the profit and loss, the mortgages and divorce and missed opportunities embodied by those gilt statuettes. Then she turned to me with a tired smile. "Have you ever tasted a dewberry?" she said. "They're like blackberries, only bigger. Oh man, they're delicious." On fall days like this, she said, when she took her puppies into the woods for a run, the pig and the goats sometimes tagged along. If she wanted to, she said, she could sustain herself on wild fruit as she went—on dewberries and muscadine grapes, sand plums, hog plums, and wild persimmons—following the seasons as they wheeled through the last of the old bottomlands. "This is still big country," she said. "We can just ride and ride and never get out of the woods."

—

I think about her out there sometimes, when I'm home at night in my brownstone, and wonder what I might be willing to trade for such a life, as Beck traded in her house and first marriage and more besides. I live in Brooklyn now, where the lights burn even brighter than in Cambridge, with a coonhound at the foot of my bed who may never know what she's missing. It's too late to teach Hattie about raccoons, and I wouldn't have the patience for it anyway. But I like to think that if I had she might have done her bloodline proud. A good coonhound is born, not made, Beck says. And it's hard not to imagine what Hattie could have been, when her ears prick up and her nose traces crazy patterns through the autumn leaves. At night, when friends see her twitching her paws in her sleep, they tell me that she's chasing rabbits in her dreams. But I know better.

Low on the Hog

What a group of people we were, I thought. Why, you could cause us the greatest humiliation simply by confronting us with something we liked. Not all of us, but so many. Simply by walking up and shaking a set of chitterlings or a well-boiled hog maw at them during the clear light of day!

—Ralph Ellison, *Invisible Man*

Tim Patridge was seventeen years old and hungry for the wide world beyond Atlanta, when he first learned that you can make a silk purse out of a sow's ear. He was working at the Hyatt Regency at the time, in the kitchen of a German chef named Walter Staib. As *chef tournant*, Patridge filled in wherever he was needed—trussing a pheasant here, carving a prime rib there—leaving the delicate touches to his boss. Then one night an order arrived that reversed their roles, if only for a moment.

Sammy Davis Jr. was staying at the hotel, a waiter announced, and he wasn't interested in the regular menu. He wanted pig's ears and pig's feet for dinner, and he wanted them served on silver chafing dishes, with the Hyatt's full "celebrity service."

"Staib, he just turned to me and another black guy and said, 'You handle this one,'" Patridge remembers. "Wasn't no big deal about it: just put 'em in a pot with some onions and green peppers and boil 'em down. But that was a significant point in my life. I mean, these days I can make you a galantine of duck or a *navarin* of lamb, I can make you a *poitrine de veau* or a French peasant pâté. But I've never been ashamed of southern food since then."

Patridge tells me this story over a plate of steaming chitlins at Scholars, the restaurant—or "laboratory," as he prefers to call it—that he founded at Morris Brown College in Atlanta. It's late in the morning, and the room around us hums with expectation, a vacuum soon to be filled with the lunch rush. Waiters in tuxedo shirts, bow ties, and paisley vests move soundlessly across deep burgundy carpets, hooking table skirts onto curved buffet tables. Fresh-cut flowers and old books decorate the tables, and a grand piano, standing in the corner, awaits some student musician's limber fingers. All along the walls, above the dark oak wainscoting, Langston Hughes and Zora Neale Hurston, Louise Jones and Dizzy Gillespie, look out from faux naïf portraits, reminding students how much has changed since 1881, when Morris Brown became the first American college to be founded by blacks for blacks.

It's Friday, so the waiters are setting out a full silver fish service and wheeling in Patridge's ice sculpture of a tugboat. But chitlins are emphatically not of the sea. To make them, Patridge took the large and small intestines of a hog, painstakingly scrubbed them and stripped them of their fatty inner membrane, then cooked them down with onions and garlic. Stretched out on my plate next to a hill of coleslaw, they look like pieces of old lasagna (some people call them "wrinkle steak") and give off a smell that shoulders roughly through the dining room's faint floral perfume. It's an aroma not so much of meat or excrement as of pig itself—the live animal, unwashed and uncut, charging bodily off the plate and into my nostrils. Yet the taste is surprisingly subtle: tender, musty, and slightly gummy, but inoffensive on the whole. If I pinch my nose, the pig disappears.

"Your new generation of southerners, they don't want to be seen eatin' that," Patridge says. "But it's just like anything else: you get past the smell, it's all right." I nod noncommittally, but he doesn't need encouragement. "I don't believe in soul food being particular to one race or culture," he says. "I mean, you can get *high class* and talk about 'sweetbreads' and 'organ meats' and stuff, but they're all down there with the chitlins anyway. They're all cleanin' and digestin' and filterin', too."

He's finding his groove now, voice rising and falling like a country preacher, body rolling and bobbing in his chair like a balloon on an updraft. At six feet and 225 pounds, Patridge looks less fat than well inflated, with taut cheeks, bulging eyes, and a gleaming bald pate, like a miniature version of his gut. He turned forty-eight this year but looks and acts at least five years younger than that, despite his grizzled beard. "Old folks say chitlins raise your blood pressure," he says, lowering his voice and leaning in closer, thick glasses widening his already wide eyes. Then he jerks back with a shout, chopping the air with his outstretched finger. "But you're talkin' about pure *protein* there! That's very low in fat! You put in a little bit of the *maw* to give it some body, you get a little bit of that natural *gelatin* goin', and you've got a dish that satisfies the human *soul*."

———

The world is full of people who define themselves by what they won't eat: macrobiotics, vegetarians, weight watchers, and weight lifters. But sometimes the more difficult, more audacious act is to define yourself by what you *will* eat—especially if it turns everyone else's stomach. So it is that Scandinavians eat lutefisk, Germans eat Limburger, Scots eat haggis, and little boys eat chocolate-covered ants. As a

Chinese cop put it in a recent movie, chewing on sea cucumbers while talking to his white partner: "You want to be Chinese? You got to learn to eat nasty stuff."

Soul food is the epitome of this phenomenon. Not so long ago chitlins and pig's feet were slave rations—the parts the master threw away while he ate the cuts "high on the hog." Though most blacks and poor whites kept a taste for such food long after the Civil War, others came to see it as a kind of self-abasement. Then in the 1960s black activists briefly, thrillingly, turned history's tables. What were once the master's leftovers, they declared, were now soul food: dishes so earthy, so rich in shared suffering and redemption, that only blacks could truly appreciate them.

Soul food was a form of culinary alchemy, transmuting humiliation into self-respect, exile into ethnic pride. But its magic was unstable at best. First there were the practical drawbacks of eating the fatty pork dishes that increasingly dominated soul food: a third of all blacks suffer from high blood pressure, and they have a 50 percent greater chance of dying from heart disease than whites do. Then there were changes in taste: as blacks joined the middle class, they wanted to live high on the hog as well. Then, finally, culinary scholars began to redefine African American cooking itself.

By now soul food has been knocked about for so

long by separatists and assimilationists, pummeled by so many qualifiers and redefinitions, that it sometimes seems out for the count. Most soul food restaurants have gone the way of the Afro, and many blacks never refer to soul food anymore, much less eat it. Yet today the odor of these chitlins does more than cut through the room's cloying perfume; it revives the old arguments like a bottle of smelling salts. Does soul food honor slave history or just trivialize it? Does it enrich black culture or misrepresent it? The further the tradition fades, the more urgent those questions become.

Even in Patridge's laboratory, there are no easy answers. While he raves about pig's ears and wrinkle steak until they seem fit for the menu on the space shuttle, the other black cooks on staff have kept their distance this morning. Earlier I walked in on Michael Chaires, the dreadlocked young executive chef, sneaking some chitlins from the pot. "You got to be in the mood for it," he mumbled, shooting me a guilty look. Then he took a bite anyway. "Oh, man!" he said. "I guess I'm not in the mood for it today."

—

As I write, three African American cookbooks are sitting on the desk beside me. *What Mrs. Fisher Knows About Old Southern Cooking* is the first African American cookbook ever published: a collection of household recipes, published in 1881, by a former slave from South Carolina. *The Welcome Table*, published in 1995, is a nostalgic gathering of traditional recipes by Jessica Harris, the country's foremost scholar of African American cooking. *A Taste of Heritage*, published in 1998, contains nouvelle soul food recipes from twelve of the country's leading black chefs. Though they cover the same field, the three books don't have much in common. From fried grits to terrapin stew, peanut soup to venison patties with wild mushroom sauce, they wind their way from country cooking to haute cuisine with only a few shared landmarks. What, then, is authentic soul food?

Thirty-five years ago the answer seemed obvious. "In the Confederate states, three cultural and gastronomic styles blended," *The American Heritage Cookbook* declared in 1964. "Latin, Anglo-Saxon, and Negro—romance, tradition, and primitive strength." But that simple outline now seems simple-minded, or worse. Nearly every bit of conventional wisdom about slave food is wrong, it turns out, beginning with what the first slaves brought from Africa.

The people whom Europeans met in West Africa were accomplished farmers, scholars have shown. They had fields of millet, sorghum, rice, and yams, patches of pumpkins, turnips, cabbage, and eggplant. For meat they had wild game and the inexhaustible sea; for dessert, wild lemons, oranges, dates, figs, and palm wine. On occasion they even found truffles— bigger than rabbits, according to one source—and carefully roasted them or cooked them in broth.

Once in the Americas, the slaves added more than "primitive strength" to southern cooking, they helped invent it from the ground up. Okra, sorghum, sesame, and watermelon all came to the Americas with the slaves (it was a two-way street: the Americas gave Africa potatoes, peanuts, chilies, corn, and tomatoes), and only slaves had the expertise to grow and prepare them. The same was true of rice, which Africans had cultivated for three thousand years. By the eighteenth century plantation owners were deliberately buying slaves from rice-growing parts of Africa, and rice was the backbone of Carolina cooking. In the nineteenth century, a rice grower named Elizabeth Allston Pringle acknowledged that "only the African race could have made it possible or profitable to clear the dense cypress swamps and cultivate rice in them by a system of flooding the fields from the river by canals, ditches, or floodgates."

As in cultivation so in preparation, slaves were the guiding intelligence behind Southern food, waging their campaign on two fronts: the slave cabin and the big house. At home they struggled to make decent dishes from meager monthly rations—"eight pounds of pickled pork . . . often tainted," as Frederick Douglass wrote, and "one bushel of Indian meal, unbolted, of which quite fifteen percent was more fit for pigs than for men." After a grueling day's work, a slave might plant greens in a communal garden or hunt for opossums, raccoons, and other nocturnal animals. These could then be thrown into the stew-pot, as part of African recipes adapted to American ingredients: sweet potatoes substituted for African yams, chilies for melegueta peppers, cornmeal for millet and sorghum.

At the big house, meanwhile, slaves invariably prepared the master's meals. Though the mistress often supervised the baking and preserving, she rarely cooked a dish herself. "Those African-American women left their thumbprint on every dish they cooked," historian Karen Hess writes in the afterword to *What Mrs. Fisher Knows About Old Southern Cooking.* "They did the cooking; it's as simple as that." A black cook, instinctively following African recipes, might add a little okra to chicken soup to thicken it, some black-eyed peas and bacon to rice to give it more taste and body, or cayenne pepper to almost anything to give it some zing. "The Negroes are born cooks, as other less favored beings are born poets," a gourmet named Charles Gayarré mused back in the 1880s, in *Harper's New Monthly Magazine.* "The African [has] gradually evolved into an artist of the highest degree of excellence, and [has] created an art of cooking for which he should deserve to be immortalized."

All southern cooking, one could almost say, is largely African American cooking. But soul food is something more specific, more self-conscious. Leafing through the three cookbooks beside me, I can see a pattern gather and then unravel, like the stitching on an old sampler. When Abby Fisher wrote her cookbook, soul food didn't exist yet. Though Fisher was an ex-slave, what she knew about old southern cooking was what any good southern cook knew: fried chicken, oyster croquettes, and Maryland beat biscuits; chow-chow, custard pie, and sweet pickle peaches. (Fisher won two medals at the 1880 San Francisco Mechanics' Institute Fair, her book proudly notes, for her pickles, sauces, jellies, and preserves.)

A century later *The Welcome Table* winnows out those dishes in favor of ones that smack more pungently of slavery. Jessica Harris doesn't like the term *soul food*, but her cookbook could well be its bible: chitlins, okra fritters, cornmeal mush, and gospel bird are all here. "Our way with food," she writes, "combines the improvisational impulses that gave the world jazz with the culinary techniques of the African continent. It combines the African taste for the piquant with the American leftovers from sorrow's kitchens." But though Harris explores the full breadth of African American cooking elsewhere, this menu is mostly low on the hog. The French, Spanish, and English dishes that slaves adapted, as Louis Armstrong did Bach fugues, find little welcome here.

A Taste of Heritage tries to redress the balance, to reclaim some of the old plantation elegance. "We have a mission, however paradoxical, to make the established 'soul food' more respectable," the authors write. "Let's face it, some African-Americans are no longer eating chitterlings and other pig's offal because of painful memories. . . . They appreciate their culinary heritage, but they refuse to be defined by it." Though *A Taste of Heritage* has its share of down-home recipes, it also reaches for dishes no slave ever cooked—in the big house or elsewhere: "Chilled Georgia Peach and Sun-Dried Cherry Soup," for instance, or "Grilled Salmon Fillets with Cilantro Vinaigrette." It's the end of a cycle, you might say, from southern food to soul food and back again—from slaves inventing dishes for their masters to blacks reclaiming and reinventing those dishes for themselves. But surely something is being lost.

Ten years ago, when Harris published her first book on African American cooking, she wrote that she hoped it might "fix the taste of cornbread, beans, collard greens, okra, chiles, molasses, and rum on our tongues for generations to come." But these days she eats such things only on New Year's Eve. The rest of the year she prefers salads. Dishes like chitlins have become more "totemic" than dietary, she says. "We keep them for the memory as much as anything else. It's like the lamb shank at a Jewish Seder: everybody doesn't eat it, but it's there."

—

On a breezy April evening, with the day's embers still glowing in the city's sidewalks and buildings, Patridge trudges down a concrete staircase, leaving the hushed confines of Scholars for the Morris Brown Football Stadium. He'll make this quarter-mile trip ten times in the next two hours, always on foot, as he directs simultaneous dinners at both locations. "When I was the director of operations at Epcot Center, I put a pedometer on one time," he says, wiping the sweat from his eyes. "By the end of the day, I'd done nine miles." He stops and leans against a wall, chest heaving. "I'm doin' my jogging here, then later I'll do my weight training in the kitchen."

Tonight's events typify Patridge's two worlds. Over at the stadium, built for the 1996 Olympics, 150 athletes are attending an awards dinner ("The football team was three and eight," Patridge quips, "so this ought to be short"). At Scholars, meanwhile, Sigma Pi Phi, one of the city's most distinguished black fraternal organizations, is having their monthly meeting. At the stadium, the menu is pulled pork, baked beans, and coleslaw; at Scholars it's seared salmon with caper sauce and wild rice. Soul food over here, plantation finery over there: the path between them is steep and circuitous, but Patridge doesn't mind the trip. You might say he's been preparing for it all his life.

His father was a country boy from Fayetteville, raised by sharecroppers. His mother was a city girl from Covington, a professional cook who had traveled to thirty-three states. On his father's side every food was tied to some person, season, or life event: there was reunion chicken (crispy and tender, because all the wives were competing) and funeral chicken (soggy and burnt, because the cooks were too sad to care). There were Aunt Lily's preserves and Aunt Cora's cakes and Aunt Ethel's chitlins, a week in the cleaning. On his mother's side, dinner was more unpredictable. "She was good at inventing dishes," Patridge says. "She used to make this thing called heavenly rice; it had rice, crushed pineapple, whipped cream, and sugar. . . . Oh, man!"

For most of Tim's life his mother worked for the Atlanta school cafeterias. Then, when he was in junior high, she opened Patridge's Dinette, on Bankhead Highway. Between there and the farm, her son learned an equal love for home and commercial cooking, plain food and its transformation. When he turned twelve his father handed him a knife and told him to go kill a hog. When he was fourteen his mother handed him a spatula and told him to make country-fried steak for her customers.

By the late 1960s, when Patridge went to Morris Brown, Atlanta was full of soul brothers and soul sisters, wearing soul combs and doing soul hand-shakes. "Everything was getting souled," as Harris puts it, "sometimes by African Americans, sometimes not." Whether the fashion called for Technicolor dashikis or denim jackets and work boots, Patridge fit right in. But his goals were hardly trendy. He wanted to be a doctor, he says, though anything ambitious might have done. So he found work at a veterans' hospital. "I started out as a dishwasher and pretty soon moved up to pot washer. Then I started delivering patient trays, and I saw those guys comin' back from Vietnam. It was like, 'Oh no, I can't do this.' " Soon after that he took a job as a cook at an airport restaurant and never looked back.

On paper, at least, the career that followed rose as unerringly as a guided missile: from the airport to the Hyatt to the Ritz, from line cook to sous chef to program director. Patridge was the first black executive chef at Callaway Gardens, a resort in Pine Mountain, Georgia; the first black *garde-manger* at the Ritz; and the first black president of the Atlanta chapter of the American Culinary Federation. He became a certified executive chef and a member of the American Academy of Chefs, always putting CEC and AAC after his name, even on a pamphlet on barbecue.

But Patridge was bent on more than exploding racial barriers. He was after a "global concept of food," he says, one that could reconcile the disparate elements of his culinary education. After so many years of separating soul food from haute cuisine, spoonbread from soufflé, he wanted to find their common denominators. Rather than settle in at a single restaurant, therefore, he began to travel. He went on cultural exchanges to Russia, eastern Europe, and the

Caribbean, where he met his future wife. He took jobs with the Atlanta Olympics and the Smithsonian, studied the historical connections between jambalaya and cassoulet. Finally, in 1997 he landed near the shores of the Magic Kingdom itself, as one of the first black executives at Epcot Center.

It seemed a fitting climax to his career, an almost eerie amalgamation of his interests. Where better to demonstrate culinary affinities than at Epcot's international pavilions? Yet at Epcot something in him splintered. Finding cultural common ground had seemed a noble idea, until he was surrounded by puppets singing "It's a Small World." With his family still in Atlanta, and Disney leaving little room for improvisation, he began to yearn for his old double life again. "If I'd been a little younger, they could have robotized me," Patridge says, "turned me into a Stepford wife." Instead, six weeks after arriving, he resigned. Then, like an escape pod jettisoned from a flaming rocket, he tumbled home to his family again—back in the arms of sweet Georgia.

He lives on a small farm now, seventeen miles from downtown Atlanta. His children all bear Yoruba names—Devika, Adisa, Ajani—and the two eldest go to Morris Brown, as he did. On weekdays he still hosts cooking shows on TV, prepares continental cuisine at Scholars, and proudly lists the honorifics after his name. But on weekends, when he cooks for his family, he leaves his ego—and haute cuisine—in the cupboard. "I know my daughter doesn't eat carrots, my son doesn't like okra, and my wife likes her chicken fried, not boiled," he says. "That's what southern cooking is all about—traditions and family —not someone tryin' to be the number one biscuit maker."

Tonight, lurching into the Scholars kitchen after his climb from the stadium, Patridge looks winded and sweaty, but at ease with his contradictions. "Mr. Chaires!" he shouts between gasps. "How's that dinner coming?" Then he walks over and shows the cooks how to arrange it: a scoop of wild rice to one side, a broiled tomato with Parmesan to the other, a broiled salmon fillet to complete the triangle. "You got to lay these with the tail inside," Patridge says, placing an asparagus spear across the plate with his big paws. Then he spoons capers over the fish and crowns it with half a lemon wrapped in lace.

Out in the dining room the Sigma Pi Phi men are having cocktails, discussing politics and art with the easy refinement of diplomats. Their suits are finely tailored and cut from exquisite cloth, their hair swept back and shot through with silver, their eyeglasses held loosely in their hands. "I knew all about these guys when I was growing up," Patridge whispers, watching them through a small window in the kitchen door. "They've got a couple of college presidents out there, a state senator, and a former superintendent of schools."

Yet even here, at the apex of the black elite, the menu can't shrug off the old ambivalence. Patridge's dinners are all on their plates and ready to be served when Chaires staggers over, carrying a tray piled high with fried chicken. "What do you want me to do with this?" he says. Patridge just stares at him: he forgot about the chicken. Glancing over at me, he slowly shakes his head. "I told them it didn't go with the salmon," he says. "But they got to have it anyway. Fried chicken every time."

Through the window, under the soft lights and softer music, the men are taking their seats, shaking out their linen napkins and looking about expectantly. Do I see a glint of defiance in their eyes? Maybe they're reluctant to give up on soul food, having worked so hard to reclaim it in the sixties. Or maybe, after so long in the minefields of race, where every symbol can explode in your face and every misstep draws friendly fire, they just want to eat their favorite dish in peace. "Just pile the chicken up in big bowls and put it in the middle of the table, Mr. Chaires," Patridge says, laughing despite himself. "That's the way they'll want it."

—

Late one night, after another twelve-hour day at Scholars, Patridge takes me on a ride through Atlanta's old black districts. "When I was a kid, all these places had special names," he says, surveying the sagging storefronts next to his old street, their boarded windows flickered by neon and tattered posters. "There was Lightnin' and Beaver Slide, Mechanicsville and Vine City." His father drove an Ace cab, he says, and on Saturdays he'd take Tim along to help the ladies with their groceries. Tim got to know the whole city that way, and to like most of it. But his favorite place—the true heart of black Atlanta—was Sweet Auburn.

Just a few blocks from the center of town, Auburn Avenue was lined with restaurants, barbershops, private clubs, and funeral homes. During the day people walked the streets in their Sunday best, stopping to gossip at the Silver Moon barbershop or to eat at B. B. Beamon's and Henry's Grill. By night Jackie Wilson, James Brown, Major Lance, and Little Richard were on stage at clubs like Zanzibar and the Royal Peacock. "I saw Bobby Blue Bland at the Peacock when I was just sixteen," Patridge remembers. "But don't ever let my mom know that."

It was on Auburn Avenue that Martin Luther King spent his childhood, playing pickup games at the YMCA and checking out stacks of books every Saturday from the public library. And it was here that he returned in 1960 to be pastor of Ebenezer Baptist Church, as his father and maternal grandfather had been before him. These streets, where all of black society gathered on the same sidewalks to reach for the same elusive prize, were the true inspiration for King's dream.

But tonight, cruising down Auburn Avenue, it's hard to recognize his vision in these ruins. B. B. Beamon's has long since gone dark, its windows painted with a mural of the neighborhood's history, and where Henry's Grill used to be, there is a nameless Caribbean restaurant. The Royal Peacock is a rap club now, and the Masonic lodge and Odd Fellows hall lean like pallbearers along the street. "*That's* the only thing keeping this place alive," Patridge says, pointing to a dim white shape lit by spotlights off the side of the road. "Martin's coffin." In 1980 then-president Jimmy Carter signed a law declaring the neighborhood a national historic site. In the years since, the National Park Service has bought twelve acres and twenty-four homes here, including King's neighbors' houses, and a new church has risen along the avenue, angled toward King's shining tomb like a shepherd toward a star, attracting some twelve hundred tourists and pilgrims every day.

If Auburn Avenue survives, it does so in the shadow of a double irony: for if King's death keeps the neighborhood alive, it was his life's work that nearly finished it off. Before the civil rights movement, nearly every city had an all-black business district, built and maintained by its captive audience: the south side of Chicago, the north side of Milwaukee, Beale Street in Memphis, Farish Street in Jackson, Greenwood in Tulsa. As soon as white businesses opened their doors to blacks, however, black businesses began to shut theirs for good. Affluent blacks fled for the suburbs, leaving only the poor and working class behind. Black shopkeepers began to look for newer digs, and "urban renewal" leveled what they left behind. (A highway now crosses Auburn Avenue, and desolate apartments stand where a square mile of houses used to be.) "Desegregation deconstructed the African American community," says Sterling Plumpp, professor of African American studies at the University of Illinois at Chicago. "It used to be, if I owned a soul food place, I could expect the crème de la crème of black society to come through—you'd get the mayor and the aldermen and celebrities like Lou Brock. But now, in the inner cities, everyone is basically poor. That whole cross section—doctor, lawyer, opera star, blues singer—it's gone."

Like the black community itself, soul food never left Sweet Auburn. Ace Barbecue Barn still sits near the avenue, and dozens of places like it dot the city, offering the same black-eyed peas, the same peach pie. But theirs is a degraded form of the art—soul food without the soul. It substitutes fatback and boiling grease for the roots, greens, and fragrant stews that slaves once favored at home. It's a product of lengthening workdays and two-income families rather than loving hours in the kitchen, of a society ever more addicted to speed, the great homogenizer.

"At one time, I don't care how poor you were, you gathered them around the dinner table," says Leah Chase, chef and owner of Dooky Chase, a fixture of Creole cooking in New Orleans since 1939. "Now they get a leg and a thigh and a biscuit and sit around the TV."

Well past midnight, Patridge and I pull up at one of the birthplaces of fast food in America—and the graveyard, perhaps, of soul food. Founded in 1928, the Varsity now cranks out 6,500 hamburgers and more than two miles of hot dogs a day. On a typical football Saturday it serves forty-five thousand customers. Until 1964 blacks weren't allowed inside, except as fry cooks, but now they're close to a majority. Some come for the retro decor—the neon lights, streamlined steel counters, and red-and-yellow walls—or to watch the workers peel potatoes from fifty-pound boxes. Others like the gift shop and the autographed pictures of celebrities like Nipsy Russell, who was a "curb boy" here in the fifties. Still others come for something more basic: sitting on cheap patio furniture, watching TVs suspended from the ceiling, you can almost feel as if you're eating at home—as long as you can ignore the food.

"Tim," I say, choking down a mouthful of grainy chili and mealy meat, "this . . . is not a good hot dog." He chuckles nervously, glancing around to see if anybody heard me. He knows I'm right, of course—as a friend of his puts it: "Every time I drive by the

Varsity I order two hot dogs, an order of onion rings, and a bottle of barbiturates"—but that doesn't mean he likes to hear it said out loud. When a cop walks by a little later to lock the doors, Patridge takes the opportunity to hustle me outside.

Back in the car, he shudders theatrically. "I had to get you out of there *fast*," he says. "I was afraid the earth was going to open under us: *blasphemer!*"

—

Two miles from the Varsity, on a patch of land that was once a residential area, Atlanta's other great attraction rises like a rose-colored memory—like a promise that history's messy subdivisions will one day be razed clean, replaced with a brighter, shinier past. When it was built in 1993 and 1994, to house the Olympics and then the Atlanta Braves, Turner Field was designed to look old-fashioned. But beneath its brick walls and outsize colonial fixtures there beats a modern heart. Under the bleachers and quaint concession stands, delivery trucks barrel down an interior road and electronic gates snap open and shut, forklifts whir from crate to crate, and beer is pumped, by the thousands of gallons, to spigots secreted in the concrete above.

It's here, on a fever-hot Sunday morning, on my last day in Atlanta, that the future of American food will be on display—or at least one version of it, courtesy of *Cooking Light* magazine. Ten white tents have been set up for cooking demonstrations, and sales booths entice the health conscious—thirty thousand of them, the promoters predict. There are booths where you can measure your body fat and booths where you can book "healthy vacations"; a tent devoted to giving away granola bars; and an artificial cliff face for rock climbing. "That's Graham Kerr over there," Patridge says, pointing to the "Healthy Choices" pavilion. "He used to be the Galloping Gourmet, but he got too *fat* to gallop—had to slow down to a *trot*. So now he's cooking light."

Patridge has been asked to give a fifteen-minute presentation on light southern cooking, though he says, "In the South, 'light' just means a little less *lard*." So he's brought the ingredients for some salmon cakes. All around us the other presentations are in full swing. Skinny white audience members head off to hear skinny white cooks bemoan the evils of heart disease, the pleasures of arugula. When Patridge barrels through them, streaming with sweat and lugging a battered ice chest, they scatter like gazelles before a rhinoceros. "You'll notice," he says, grinning, "that I'm the only African American out here."

If the Varsity is the Scylla of soul food, surely this is its Charybdis. Racial politics will cycle and change; black families will grow tired of takeout and return to the kitchen; but the slow corruption of recipes can take decades to undo. Oleo for butter here, turkey bones for ham hocks there, a teaspoon of salt where the taste used to be: substitute or skimp on enough ingredients, and people will forget why they ever ate such things. It's hard to believe in the richness of African American cooking while eating a plate of boiled collards and cottage cheese.

Patridge, luckily, is an old hand at navigating such straits. Ten minutes after we arrive, he rises up on stage in his white, double-breasted chef's jacket: a god of plenty, come to lead us from this blistering desert. "Good afternoon, ladies and gentlemen, on this *hot* day," he begins. "We'll all be lighter when we leave." While the audience titters, he looks around at the bare counter and meager implements, the chunk of cold salmon and handful of eggs. "I knew that there'd be nothing but light cooking here today," he says. "So I went down to the Varsity last night and got loaded *up*—you know, so it wouldn't be too much of a *shock* to my system. I even brought some canola oil." He turns his lips down at the corners as if vastly impressed with himself. "But I had to go out and *buy* it."

Beside me, a middle-aged woman in jogging shorts and a platinum blond wig sits upright and peers at the stage, not sure if she's hearing right. But Patridge is already off on another riff. He talks about salmon and how southerners first tasted it in a can—"ain't no salmon swimmin' up the Chattahoochee." He says he's all for light cooking, as long as you can eat twice as much of it. And he points out that southerners are no strangers to haute cuisine. "Look here," he says, pointing to the lone black man in the audience. "If I showed a southerner some polenta made with Parmesan, what would he call it?"

The man frowns for a second and then breaks into a grin: "Cheese grits!"

Then Patridge points to a white woman in the front row. "And if I mix this grape jelly with some ketchup and apple-cider vinegar, what would you call it?"

She looks at him quizzically. "Sweet-and-sour sauce?"

"*That's right!*"

By now there's a crowd inside the tent. Stragglers come in from the sidewalk to see what all the commotion is about, and defectors are arriving from the lecture next door. The old lady beside me is having a hard time breathing, she's laughing so hard, and I can feel a giddy, subversive spirit building around me. "Let me show you the *professional* way to separate this," Patridge says, holding up an egg. He smacks it against the counter and cracks it open into his hand, letting the white stream through his fingers. When all that's left is the yolk, he throws it over his shoulder into the trash. "That's the cookin' light part," he says. Next he mashes the egg white into the salmon, adds some flour and seasonings, and forms four little cakes. "You know sometimes when you go to a restaurant and you see egg whites on the menu?" he asks, placing the cakes on a griddle. "Anyone here ever eat those egg whites?" Not a hand is raised. "I knew it," Patridge says, his sermon complete. "We're at the *wrong* show."

Watching him up there on stage, so alone and yet so fully in command, so out of place and yet so eager to connect, I can't help but think how far we've come—both forward and back. Not so long ago Patridge's grandfather was a sharecropper, devoted to making the best from the least, whether turning a sow's ear into a silken dish or a slave's life into something more human. But history and hard-won prosperity have contrived to turn that gift upon itself. These days the older our country grows, the weaker our traditions seem to become; the more varied our food, the more predictable our cooking. It's a hall of mirrors we've wandered into, where hog maws are a rare delicacy and the world's richest people eat the world's blandest food. Any eighteenth-century time traveler, transported here in search of wonders, might well react as Patridge did, looking out across this sea of dissatisfied faces: "We're at the *wrong* show."

After Patridge's talk, the crowd drifts away—some to other talks, others to the "Free Stuff" tent for more granola bars. But an elderly woman, pale and pinched by one too many diets, stays behind. "Can I ask you a question?" she says when the others have cleared out. "Are you from around here?"

Patridge looks down into her glimmering little face and chuckles. "Born and raised, ma'am, born and raised."

She squints at him a moment longer, as if still unsure, and then curls her mouth into a smile. "I knew it," she says, sidling up to him like a bookie with a hot tip. "I'll tell you one thing, though: Most of these other folks around here are Yankees."

Patridge shakes his head as she wanders toward the exit. "I wish you were right," his eyes seem to say. "I wish you were right."

The Rolley Holers

Like most men who aren't much good at sports, I spent a good deal of my childhood making up Olympic events, just to have something to be best at. Mine weren't the usual obstacle courses, bicycle jumps, or beanbag tosses. They were cryptic and personal and hard to re-create—more gestures, really, than games. I might cross my fingers in a certain pattern, say, and use them to flick a penny across the room, or shoot a rubber band over my shoulder with my toes—it didn't matter, as long as I could do it and no one else I knew had ever tried. After an hour or so of dedicated practice, having achieved a kind of cockeyed perfection, I'd stop and pat myself on the back. "Right now," I'd tell myself, "you're better at this than anyone else in the world."

I was probably wrong. Every backyard Ping-Pong player thinks he's the king of the world, until he plays a Chinese exchange student. Every family Scrabble champ believes the game can be played no better, until he hears that the world champion scored seven hundred points in a round, closing out with "qi." There are five billion people living on the planet, most of them with some idle time on their hands. Somewhere, in an alleyway in Calcutta or a forest clearing in Papua New Guinea, some boy has probably discovered my weird little gestures, practiced them assiduously, and beaten every one of my records. To me they were just a way to pass the time. But to him they were a way of life.

I thought about that not long ago, standing under a hickory tree in the hills of northern Tennessee. It was a cool September evening, with the darkness just beginning to well up out of the hollows, and the crowd I'd joined was so hushed and watchful that I could hear the forest chitter and chime with katydids and field crickets. We were gathered around a rectangular court of fine umber dust, sheltered by a pavilion and illuminated by spotlights. Four men in jeans and T-shirts were on the court, slouched with hands in pockets or sitting on their heels. If not for the crowd, you might have taken them for roadies waiting to set up equipment on an empty dance floor. But then one of them knelt down and reached his right arm out in front of him. For just a second I could see a pale gray marble, held loose and precarious in his curled, upturned fingers. Then it was gone, flying twenty feet or so across the yard, hitting another marble dead-on and spinning to a stop in its target's place.

It was an impossible shot—one I could never reliably make—but no big deal to the shooter. He shuffled over, picked up his marble, and flicked it toward a shallow, marble-size depression in the dust two feet away. This was more of a putt than a drive, and the marble rolled rather than flew. Still, it headed straight for its nesting place, skidding on backspin until it settled in with a final fidget, like a fat man getting ready for a double feature.

The shooter's name was Jack Tinsley, and he'd been sinking shots like these all day. Like all the other players here at the fifteenth annual Standing Stone Marbles Tournament, he was a local boy, born and raised not twenty miles from here. A plumber, builder, and sometime tobacco farmer, Jack had the furtive, half-wild look of a mountain man—bony shoulders, unkempt hair, Rip Van Winkle beard— and he seemed uncomfortable in bright light. Between shots he held his elbow and avoided people's eyes, as liable to trip over his own feet as over his words if you asked him a question. It was only when he crouched down to shoot that his body seemed to untangle, to move with the fluid, unconscious grace of a professional athlete.

Jack was a fanatic rolley holer. This is not to say that he belonged to some odd evangelical sect, but simply that he loved to play a game called rolley hole. Rolley holers play in teams of two, sinking their marbles in holes and trying to prevent their opponents from doing the same. There are three holes in all, one at either end of the court and one in the middle. The first team to work its way down the court and back three times, sinking its marbles in each hole in succession, wins the game. You might say rolley hole is a combination of marbles, croquet, and golf, but that does it little justice. It's a game that demands dexterity, an intuitive grasp of spatial relations, and a subtle command of field strategy. It's a game that rewards fanaticism. As one molecular-biologist-turned-rolley-hole-aficionado put it, "Rolley hole is to other marble games as chess is to checkers."

By those terms Jack was a grand master, yet he had never won this tournament. Anywhere else he might have been a local legend by now, but on the upper Cumberland, marble virtuosos are as common as raccoons. For generations those hills have been swept by rolley hole fevers as intense as religious revivals. They've seen players murdered by their rivals and border wars break out between factions from Kentucky and Tennessee. They've seen people hike miles in search of the hardest flint and craftsmen spend hours grinding it down in pursuit of the perfect marble.

This is the story of how the rolley holers came down from the mountains one day to challenge the best marble players in the world. It's a story about a gonzo folklorist who helped keep a tradition alive when the whole notion of tradition was starting to ring hollow. But mostly it's about an old and oddly entrancing game—one that has earned its players' consuming devotion, though it's as peculiar, in its way, as shooting rubber bands over your shoulders with your toes.

—

The upper Cumberland River flows from northern Tennessee into southern Kentucky, dipping and rolling through narrow bottomlands and high beech-wood forests, across the limestone highlands that encircle Nashville like a great amphitheater, stopping just shy of bluegrass and coal country. The land here is as stingy with resources as it is profligate with beauty, and making a living from it has never been easy. After more than two centuries the towns still look makeshift—the houses lean along the roadsides as if dropped there by a passing tornado—and folks can be so understated, they hardly talk at all. Even the local barbecue joints don't fool around. Not for them the dry rub and pit roast, tenderloin and sweet sauce. They prefer their pork sliced thin, with the bone still in it, then grilled tough as shoe leather. A swab of acrid orange grease, a piece of white bread, and voilà! Though no one here would ever say that word.

People with tastes like these don't seem the types

for a kids' game. Then again, maybe that's why they're better at it than anyone else. In most places people have lost patience with low-tech toys. Basketball players wear advanced polymers; Frisbees are tested in NASA wind tunnels; Rollerbladers streak past on titanium bearings, their bodies armored like tech warriors. But a marble is hard to accessorize. Its geometry is pure as Euclid, its physics merciless. It takes a mind of flint, Wallace Stevens might have written, to master rolley hole.

Once upon a time, the country was full of people with such minds, and most of them played with marbles. The Zuñi hid them in wooden tubes and made people guess where they were; the Shoshoni juggled them; the Tewa threw them at targets; and most other Native Americans used them as dice. Even the ancient mound builders found time for simple games. Beneath most of their massive funerary earthworks, they buried at least one "chunkee stone": a chiseled disk of quartz, four to six inches wide and slightly concave on both faces. Not yet a marble, perhaps, but well on its way.

One November morning, just outside of Little Kansas, Oklahoma, I watched twenty or thirty Cherokees play a game called Cherokee marbles. They were full-bloods, for the most part, with jet black hair, squat bodies, and flat, chiseled features, and it wasn't hard to imagine them back a thousand years, playing with chunkee stones. More than anything, though, their game reminded me of rolley hole.

Like rolley holers, Cherokee players split up into teams of two and try to sink marbles on a yard with shallow holes (a Cherokee yard has five holes instead of three). And in both games players can knock each other's marbles out of position only once at each hole. The differences are mostly a matter of scale: instead of a carefully tended, twenty-by-forty-foot court, the Cherokee play on a huge, scraggly meadow surrounded by old tires; instead of real marbles, they use pool balls. "We used to make 'em ourselves," one of the players told me, "but they broke too easy."

I could see the problem. Everywhere I looked players were rearing back like demented shot-putters, hurling their balls around hard enough to crack skulls. At the far end of the field, a player named Isaac Youngbird was balanced on one leg like an ungainly pelican, his Fu Manchu mustache whipping in the wind, waiting to see if his shot hit home. When it missed, he jumped up and down and screamed, "Shit!" The effect was both playful and deadly serious, like the lacrosse matches that Creek and Choctaw warriors once staged as substitutes for war. This was marbles, against all odds, made visceral.

Both rolley holers and Cherokee marblers like to say the Native American version came first—if only to give their games a more ancient pedigree. But it's easier to imagine it the other way around. Before the Trail of Tears, the Cherokee lived in eastern

Tennessee and the Carolinas and were famous for adopting European ways: they wore trousers and built frame houses, invented an alphabet and published their own newspapers. Perhaps, moved by some ancestral memory of chunkee stones, they adopted rolley hole as well. Then they put it on steroids.

Of course, that still begs the question: Where did rolley hole come from? Marble games have been played in Europe since before the Romans. But though games similar to rolley hole, known as three holes, are still played in Australia and England, rolley hole seems to be a purely American invention. Like gospel or gumbo, it's a compound of memory and necessity. Somewhere in the Appalachians, it's tempting to think, a frontiersman must have woken up one morning with a hankering for golf. Putters, drivers, and immaculate lawns being hard to come by, he made do with the next best thing: marbles.

—

Marble maker Randall Dulworth is close to eighty now—he still takes his first car, a 1929 Model A, out for the occasional putt around Livingston, Tennessee —but he remembers when marbles were a countywide obsession. When I visited his garage, he held up two creamy specimens from the twenties: dented, fissured, but patinaed by generations of hands. "I made 'em when I was yea high," he said, stretching out a hand at waist level. "They've seen many a battle."

Like pneumonia, marble fever was always a passing

state, a seasonal disease. In late summer, when the crops were laid by and the weeds beaten back, locals were granted a rare gift of absolute leisure, their days long and honey golden, the tobacco reaching lazily toward the sun. It was then, with the earth stuck in idle and the hours coasting from August to Indian summer, that players dusted off their old shooters and wandered back to the marble yards. After months of grim purpose and hard labor, the game's pointlessness must have been a kind of balm, its circularity the ideal relief from all that earnest forward motion.

In Dulworth's day half a dozen games were played on the upper Cumberland—games like euchre, ringer, and Tennessee square. Most were equal parts skill and luck, and people never took them too seriously. If a kid ran out of marbles, he might use acorns instead. If that wasn't good enough, he'd find some other cheap replacement. One folklorist showed me a picture of two stolid German craftsmen, lying on their stomachs in bib overalls, carefully touching marbles to a grinding wheel. "Now, the hillbillies, they didn't have time for this," he said, grinning. "They'd just go out to a stream somewhere, drill a hole in a rock, drop a stone in it, and wait about six months. When they came back, the river would have rolled it round."

The rolley holers didn't have it that easy. Only flint could withstand their crack shooting, and no stream could shape a flint marble fast enough. For generations, therefore, rolley holers kept the locations of good flint outcroppings as secret as gold strikes. (There's no shortage of flint in the upper Cumberland—deposits of it gird the hills like a rib cage—but most of it is thin, crumbly stuff.) Once they found a good, hefty nodule, they would rough out a blank and grind it down with a bow drill, specially adapted from the ones Indians used to start fires.

Nowadays technology can speed things up, but only to a point. Dulworth still starts with pieces of local flint, in colors from alabaster to bloodred, and good rock gets scarcer every year. Yellow flint is the toughest, rolley holers say, but brown makes a harder target against the dirt of a marble yard. Red is beautiful but brittle; gray and black, sturdy but unattractive. When Dulworth has chosen his rock and struck a few sparks from it, just to make sure it's genuine, he rounds it off roughly with a chisel. Then he takes a grinding stone embedded with diamond fragments—one in which he's drilled a hemispheric hole—sets the piece of flint in the hole, and holds it up to a sander, letting the marble jiggle and spin like a ball bearing in its casing. "It'll roll about a thousand miles an hour," he says. "But when it's smooth it stops rolling: the centrifugal force needs a rough spot to grab on to."

Back when Dulworth was really cranking, he could make three marbles a day and sell every one. But little by little demand began to drop off. Beginning in the

1950s, as television and organized sports began to take the American childhood in hand, marbles passed out of players' pockets and into those of decorators and nostalgia buffs. At a collectors' show you can now sell a vintage Cracker Jack marble for $300 or a rare sulfide for $5,000 or more. But kids who can talk of "mibs" and "downsies," "aggies," "alley-taws," "biffs," and "bonces," are an even rarer commodity.

Rolley holers, being adults in a region long sheltered from popular culture, held on longer than most. "There was a kind of Darwinian thing going on up there," says Robert Cogswell, a folklorist with the Tennessee Arts Commission. "In other areas your kids play football or basketball. But up in those counties, the really great natural athletes, a lot of them were marble shooters." Well into the fifties there were tournaments throughout Kentucky, and on summer nights the private marble yards still twinkled from hilltops and valleys. But the game was too sophisticated, too hard to learn and maintain, to thrive on shortening attention spans. Year by year the armies of Little Leaguers and midget football players, satellite dishes and video arcades, marched deeper into the upper Cumberland, and year by year fewer fathers taught their boys to play. For a while, in the 1960s, a man by the name of Dumas Walker kept rolley hole alive by sheer force of personality. But when Dumas quit, the game nearly died. By the late 1970s only a handful of players was left, and all of them lived in two adjacent counties—one in Kentucky and one in Tennessee.

Like some rare animal that dines only on an equally rare shrub, rolley hole had nearly evolved itself out of existence.

—

"The part I remember," Bob Fulcher says, "the part that's burned into my brain, is comin' up on those lights behind the trees."

It was a moonless night in early June, with summer's sultry breath already rising off the highlands, and Fulcher was miles from any street lamps or houselights. He'd parked his Mazda hatchback on the shoulder of the road, as instructed, walked past the ditch and the long line of pickups, crossed the sagging barbed-wire gate, and followed the trail into the trees. It was then, knee-deep in weeds, encircled by cicadas and fluttered by moths, that he noticed it. "There was this glow," he says, "this tungsten glow coming out of the forest. And you could see men moving around in it."

Fulcher had heard about these gatherings before—as director of the Tennessee State Parks Folklife Project he heard no end of strange stories—but he'd never managed to see one. Stumbling toward the light, he remembered the first time he'd been told about rolley hole. He was at a music festival in Nashville when he came across an old rhythm-and-blues player named Bud Garrett, hunched over a weird contraption. In the 1950s Garrett had cut some records for the Excello label, but nowadays he ran a junkyard in an old black community called Free Hill, spiking his income with moonshine and other ventures. The contraption, it turned out, was a marble-making machine.

"Bud was a champion talker," Fulcher recalls. "Just unbelievable. So he very quickly evoked the name of Dumas Walker. Now Dumas had been going around for a few years saying he was the world champion of rolley hole, and Bud was a great supporter of that claim. He'd repeat it at the drop of the hat. Evidently he'd beaten Dumas one time, so by supporting the claim, he elevated himself." Unfortunately, when Fulcher sent a folklorist to check out Bud's stories, both Garrett and Walker begged off. "It was: 'Oh no, I can't play. But I'm the greatest there ever was.'" A rolley hole exhibition was organized anyhow, and Garrett managed to scratch out a marble yard for it. But on the day of the event a downpour washed everything out. Though a few players showed up, they soon faded back into the forest.

Now, two years later, emerging into the clearing at last, Fulcher had to laugh: all that mystery for so harmless a thing. "Here was this strange, manicured little space in the center of the woods," he says. "There were wood shavings and old bucket seats and ranks of chairs around it, but the yard itself was an amazing sight." The owners, Russell Collins and his brother Herman, had cleared the yard with a bull-dozer, brought up a generator, and strung it with electric lights. With white oak and red maple clustered all around, shielding out the night wind and gathering in the light, the place felt faintly ceremonial, like the scene of a harvest dance or a solstice ritual. "And then here were these men shooting marbles," Fulcher says, pausing at the memory. "And they could really shoot."

Like most small-town boys, Fulcher had played a few rounds of ringer as a kid, shooting marbles from a small circle. This was nothing like that. Rolley holers regularly had to make shots four times as long as those in ringer, and their marbles, like pool balls, had to ricochet to just the right position afterward. This was like a game of basketball with baskets thirty feet high. The locals dribbled, dunked, sank fadeaways from midcourt, then shrugged as if to say "Doesn't everyone do it like that?"

While the men played, one of them pulled out a fiddle and dug into some old-time tunes—"New Five Cents," perhaps, or "Weepin' Willow Tree." Soon the men had settled into an easy, bantering rhythm, their clicking marbles keeping time. A frog hopped across the yard, Fulcher remembers, and moths fell from the lamps in clusters. As the men moved around the court, they'd crush them casually with their heels. At one point Fulcher tried to join in the game, but he fared no better than the moths. "There was just this enormous gulf," he says, "between what a person like me could do with a marble and what they could do."

Fulcher had seen his share of dying traditions. He'd seen them bandaged and mummified, sent lurching around festivals and then stuffed back into the crypt. And he'd seen them heartbreakingly vital, pumping life into a community until a cultural vacuum bled them dry. Compared to those, rolley hole was alive and well. But for how long? These guys were the last active players in the country, and they were hardly cut out to be cultural ambassadors. Like most people on the upper Cumberland, they were shy, secretive, allergic to hype. It was no surprise that they'd kept Fulcher waiting all these years; it was a surprise they'd invited him at all.

Still, something about seeing them play set Fulcher's mind spinning like a roulette wheel. A good game, he knew, is a universal language. It's a distillate of pleasure, an elegant algorithm for squeezing the most fun from the shortest period. Once explained, it makes as much sense to an Aborigine as to a hillbilly, to an ancient Babylonian as to a modern New Yorker. "This marble thing," Fulcher began to realize, "was like a boulder sitting on top of a cliff. All it needed was a little shove, just a tiny bit of momentum, and it would be off and rolling again."

—

The first thing the rolley holers needed, Fulcher decided, was a public marble yard. But not just any old piece of dirt. "Those Tennessee farmers," Fulcher says, "they look at dirt the way other people look at fine wine." For years the best yards in Tennessee had been made with spongy loam from a farm owned by Ralph Roberts, a player whose cantankerousness was rivaled only by his skill. The soil there, in the floodplain of the Cumberland River, had a peculiar toffee color and a texture, when pounded and dusted, almost like powdered skin. In time Fulcher would cap his yard with Roberts's soil. But because he built it at Standing Stone State Park, he first used loam from the bottomland around Mill Creek—the creek that had been dammed to form Standing Stone Lake. "The park maintenance guys just put down some clay at first," he says. "But one of the rangers was kin to some players, so he knew a lot about dirt." Once the yard was roughly level, Fulcher had it groomed with a tire iron weighted by cinder blocks and fluffed up with a straw brush, just as Russell Collins used to do.

So far so good. Fulcher could probably flush twenty or thirty rolley holers out of the woods on the strength of their curiosity alone. Then again, the Monroe County Fair, just across the border in Kentucky, had been staging a rolley hole tournament every Labor Day for fifty years running, and that hadn't kept the game from nearly dying.

Fulcher needed something more than a passing novelty. He needed "to get the fever going." And for that there was only one thing: "I think it was the $400 that really jolted them awake," he says. "Over at Monroe County, they were giving away the smallest trophies I've ever seen—they probably cost them 50¢. But the $400 kind of made them sit up and take notice."

That first year the Standing Stone Marbles Tournament drew fifteen teams, with Bud Garrett playing rolley-hole blues on his beat-up Fender electric. Fulcher, on the strength of a phone call, managed to convince the *NBC Nightly News* to cover the final. But that feat of persuasion was easily outdone by Travis Cherry, a mild-mannered foreman at the local Hevi-Duty factory. In the weeks before the tournament, Cherry convinced his bosses to build three marble yards next to the factory. With the $400 dangling in front of them, the men were soon playing during coffee breaks, lunch breaks, nights, and weekends. They played so much that when players at the Honest Abe lumberyard asked to build a yard, too, the owner refused. With rolley hole around, he said, no one would get any work done.

The fever, it seemed, was taking hold. By 1982 there were twenty-five teams playing at Standing Stone; by 1987 there were thirty-two, and the final was played, with fingers numbed by cold, at three in the morning. Where hog lots and potato patches once were, marble yards began to appear, and a kind of rolley-hole grand slam circuit developed: the Dumas Walker Memorial in early August, then the Monroe

County Fair, the Watermelon Festival, and finally Standing Stone on the second weekend after Labor Day. At Amos McLerran's marble yard, in a tobacco field southeast of Moss, Tennessee, parents would gather on makeshift bleachers, collect some change in a hat, and then watch their kids play like fire to win it. Even the Army Corps of Engineers joined in, building a yard in Clay County, next to an old jogging track. "They used the wrong kind of dirt," Fulcher told me when we visited it, "so this was where the outlaw, heathen element would play. They'd sit here and shoot and make rude comments about the ladies hurrying by."

—

Another folklorist might have stopped then, with kids shooting marbles at school again and going back to their fathers' secret stashes of flint. But Fulcher is hardly your standard-issue folklorist. With his liquid blue eyes and pale, scraggy face, thick aviator glasses and lopsided grin, he seems too offbeat and easygoing to worry much about dying traditions. His voice has a kind of stoned-out geniality—one part southern drawl, one part hippie slang—and when he talks about some old-fashioned thing, he seems to both inflate it with wonder and deflate it with the gentlest prick of irony. "Boy, that is some cool stuff," he'll say. "That is really low-down."

Yet behind Fulcher's oddball manner lies a mind of quicksilver creativity and natural daring. As a young man fresh from the University of Tennessee, he first fell in love with old-time traditions through music. On weeknights he played banjo in bands with names like the Mango Boys, the New Rock Creek Ramblers, and Dr. Scantlin's Red Hot Peppers. But on weekends he headed into the hills, hungry for new material.

Guided by legends, liner notes, and half-forgotten memories, Fulcher would start by knocking on doors and bothering people in cafés. If he could scare up a banjo picker or a fiddle player, he'd convince him to lay down a few tunes then and there, on a reel-to-reel Fulcher had on loan from the Library of Congress. After two summers of this, Fulcher put together five albums' worth of traditional recordings for County Records, most of them classics: fiddle tunes by Clyde Davenport; ballads by Dee Hicks and his wife, Delta; banjo work by Virgil Anderson.

It was the mid-1970s then, and the southern string band revival was winding through the South from North Carolina, trailing fiddle bands behind it like tin cans behind a wedding car. There were folk conferences and chautauquas, music festivals and vast fieldwork projects sponsored by the Smithsonian. And everywhere a kind of earnest optimism reigned: the mantra was that these traditions just needed a little hand-holding—a new suit and a hot meal and a chuck under the chin—and they would be back on their feet again.

But though Davenport would go on to win a

National Heritage Fellowship and Anderson would play Carnegie Hall, Fulcher began to feel as if his records had missed the point. The real treasures were scattered like gold dust among the recording reels he had collected, in ragged voices and often clumsy fingers, in songs that distilled countless lazy afternoons and evenings, on front porches and at kitchen tables: a living sound track of Tennessee. It was the texture of that world, more than just its best musicians, that he wanted to help preserve.

In the fall of 1977 Fulcher moved to Nashville and took a job with the Tennessee Bureau of State Parks —the same one he has today. A year later he applied to the National Endowment for the Arts and won a grant to document folklife in Tennessee. If the "tradition bearers" needed anything, he decided, it was a good promoter. So he developed a kind of souped-up revivalism—Appalachian agitprop—yoking bedrock tradition to pure showmanship. He put together cross-cultural banjo festivals, staged an exhibition of "Dixie wrestling," booked unemplyed preachers to proselytize to festival audiences ("That turned out strange"), and hired folklorists to head into the hills as he had done. "We call him the Colonel Tom Parker of folklife programming," Robert Cogswell says. "Bobby's always got some grandiose scheme cooking that he hasn't quite revealed to the world yet."

As Fulcher worked his way deeper into the marble world, his mind began to percolate. He read up on traditions in surrounding counties and worldwide, started attending marble conventions and subscribing to marble newsletters. He consulted archaeologists and hung out with marble-playing immigrants. The rolley holers, he was convinced, were the greatest players in the world. What they needed were some worthy rivals to help them prove it.

One day, leafing through a book on marbles, Fulcher came upon a picture of an old man with a long white beard, shooting marbles from a sand-covered concrete circle. For more than four centuries, the caption said, the finest shooters in England had come to Tinsley Green for the championship of British marbles. Like rolley hole, British marbles was played mostly in two counties—Sussex and Surrey—and like rolley hole, it had a history rife with legend. There was Jim "Atomic Thumb" Longhurst, who could smash a beer mug with a single shot, and Wee Willie Wright, who was five foot two and won the championship five times. Most important, the British claimed to be the world's best players: in four hundred years no outsider had ever beaten them at their game. "When I told that to the rolley holers," Fulcher says, "it kind of got 'em fired up."

—

The first clash of American and British sharpshooters took place in the hills of the upper Cumberland in 1991. It was convened, through a joint resolution, by Fulcher and Sam McCarthy, secretary of the British

Marbles Board of Control. The British, it was agreed, would send their two greatest champions to Standing Stone to compete in the tournament and an exhibition match of British marbles. The following year the Americans would return fire, sending their six finest to England for the World Marble Championship.

Fulcher was not one to let such historical echoes go unamplified. As soon as the date was set, he scribbled out some lyrics, took a bluegrass band to a studio in Jamestown, and sent tapes to all the local radio stations. In the days before the tournament you could hear his rolley hole anthem blaring from every pickup truck and construction site, to the tune of Jimmy Driftwood's "Battle of New Orleans":

In 1991 when the British came across
The great Atlantic Ocean
Just to see who was the boss
With a pocket full of marbles and a little bit of luck
They said they'd whup old Tennessee
And tailor old Kentuck

We fired our flints and the British fired their tollies
But we hit them before they hit us
We fired once more and
We give 'em such a volley
Then we busted all their marbles
And we left them in the dust

By the morning of the tournament, Fulcher says, the upper Cumberland was gripped by a mild revolutionary fervor. But the British, truth be told, made imperfect redcoats: Barry Ray, the grandson of Atomic Thumb Longhurst, was a freelance accountant from Hereford; Paddy Graham was a retired detective with the London police department. Both were plump, gregarious, sweet-mannered men, more used to playing for pints of Butty Bach bitter on a Friday night than for their country's pride. Still, they were fine shots—British champions many times over. And to the crowds at Standing Stone they seemed as exotic as Masai warriors.

No outsider had ever won a game at Standing Stone, and few expected the British to master rolley hole in a day. British marbles, on the other hand, is relatively easy to learn: forty-nine miniature marbles are clustered together at the center of a sand-covered concrete ring, six feet in diameter. Players take turns trying to shoot the marbles off the ring without letting their shooter bounce off as well; the first team to knock off twenty-five marbles wins. For the rolley holers, used to playing with much bigger marbles, this was a bit like running a hundred-yard dash in penny loafers after training for a marathon. But the distances were a cinch, and the sand was at least a distant cousin to dirt. If there was going to be a decisive battle, everyone agreed, it would be the exhibition match.

To keep things simple, and to preserve the rolley holers' ever-delicate pride, Fulcher had them draw names from a hat to see who would play the British. When the winners of the draw were announced, the British couldn't repress a smile. They'd been trounced in the rolley hole tournament by then and broiled by the Tennessee sun like so many portobello mushrooms. Here, at last, was their chance: their opponents would be Roy Thompson and his son Nathan. Roy hadn't played rolley hole in years. Nathan was nine years old.

In those days Nathan was short and pudgy, with small, gray green eyes buried behind his cheeks like the buttons on an overstuffed chair. He was quick to blush, awkward around strangers, and so shy that he almost seemed mute. He was also, in the words of one player, "about the greatest natural-born marble player I've ever seen." From the age of four Nathan's father had taken him into the backyard and taught him how to knuckle down and shoot. By the time he was six he was going to Russell Collins's place and hustling some of the older players. Beneath that blank demeanor he seemed to possess an unerring mental compass, an inborn sense of spin, and a hickory-tough self-confidence. "When the British saw Nathan, they thought they'd have it easy," Fulcher says with a chuckle. "But everyone here knew that he was a phenomenal player."

The British won the toss, and Paddy took the break,

missing badly. Roy did a little better, but he knocked no marbles off the ring. Then Barry missed, and it was Nathan's turn. After plodding over to the ring and hitching up his baggy shorts, he bent over, reached out, and casually shot off seven in a row. "That boy obviously had a good teacher," Sam McCarthy quipped nervously over the public address system.

The next rounds were nearly identical to the first: the others mostly missing, Nathan reeling off strings of three and then seven hits, and the crowd laughing and clapping louder with every shot. Finally Barry managed to knock off six in a row himself. But before McCarthy could gloat for too long—"Now, this is how it's supposed to be played"—Nathan had slammed the door with a final sequence of five.

After less than ten minutes the score stood the British 7, the Thompsons 25. "Those British players," Fulcher says, "I guess they realized then it was time to step it up and go."

> *Well we knocked 'em out of edges*
> *And we knocked 'em through the hedges*
> *And we knocked 'em in the bushes*
> *Where the rabbits wouldn't go.*
> *We knocked 'em so far*
> *That they couldn't find their marbles*
> *And they had to buy some more*
> *Just to play the rolley hole*

I got a sledgehammer thumb and a ten-inch span
I got dust in my mouth I'm a rolley-hole man
Now I want to go to England to win the silver cup
Play for all the marbles, eat some crumpets up

In the spring of 1992, when the rolley holers arrived in London for the World Marble Championship, none of them had ever crossed an ocean before, except to fight in Vietnam. Fulcher had held a tournament to see who would go, but some of the best players simply refused to get on a plane. That left Travis Cherry, Russell Collins, and Jack Tinsley, a mining equipment salesman named Ron Barnstetter, a factory worker named Bobby Dyer, and a bulldozer operator named Junior B. Strong. On the day they left, Hevi-Duty had given them each a blue satin jacket with their names stitched in front and "Tennessee-Kentucky Sharpshooters" stitched in back.

"We got to see all the sights," Cherry says. "Buckingham Palace, Westminster Abbey, and that tower where they keep all the jewels." But as Fulcher recalls, the players spent most of the week scanning rock formations. "When we drove past Stonehenge, Junior B. said he'd like to go and cut a piece of it off to make a marble," Fulcher says. "Well, he couldn't get any there, but one of the boys did manage to take a piece of chert from the walls of Windsor Castle." When they visited a folk museum in Devon, Jack and

Junior B. split off from the tour to explore a nearby creek bed, and when they went to Brighton they forgot about fish and chips as soon as they saw the beach. "The whole thing was made of flint nodules," Fulcher says. "That about blew their minds."

Tinsley Green lies due south of London, in the old industrial town of Crawley on the border between Surrey and Sussex. In the days of Queen Elizabeth I, legend had it, a man from Surrey and a man from Sussex got into an argument over a woman. To settle the matter, they challenged each other to contests of skill—archery, wrestling, and falconry—but they always came out even. Finally they agreed to meet at Tinsley Green on Good Friday for a winner-take-all marble game. Perhaps for political reasons, no one seems to remember who won that first tournament. But since then the Tinsley Green tournament has never been canceled, except during World War II. Five circles of chipped and weathered concrete lie on the green like landing pads at some Neolithic heliport, flanked by an acre of ragged grass and overlooked by the Greyhound Pub.

Good Friday that year dawned chill and drizzly— the British answer to the Tennessee heat—but the mood managed to be festive nonetheless. Teams of waitresses and policemen, firemen and steelworkers, traded taunts over morning beer while a brass band from the local ale factory blasted marches above the gusting wind. Morris dancers pranced about, waving their handkerchiefs, trying to keep warm in their tights and flimsy white shirts, and spectators and players gathered around the pub on stilts and in Day-Glo outfits.

At nine o'clock in the morning, when thirty teams had gathered at last, the village eccentric walked to center stage, dressed in a blazing orange outfit. As CNN began its live satellite feed, he drew names from a hat for the first-round pairings. Right away the rolley holers felt outclassed, at least in one respect: "That first bunch we played, they showed up in tuxedos," Cherry says. "And they were wearin' these white masks like that guy in *The Phantom of the Opera*."

Small and lean, with an elfin face, graying hair, and crinkles around the eyes from smiling, Cherry looks like an ex–student council president, ever politic and eager to please. In a crowd addicted to understatement, he may be the most approachable and the most modest. Yet when I asked him how he figured his team's chances under the circumstances, he didn't hesitate: "Oh, you know, I expected to win." Aside from skill, he said, they had a secret weapon: knotted up in a pair of Junior B.'s wife's panty hose, safe from the eyes of customs inspectors, was a gallon of Tennessee dust, gathered from Ralph Roberts's farm and baked in the transformer ovens at Hevi-Duty. Now, hunched over against the rain, glancing nervously at their masked opponents, the rolley holers reached in and rubbed it into their hands.

"That dirt, to us, is like the chalk that pool players use," Cherry explained. "You put it on your hands, you get a better release."

As it turned out, they hardly needed the leg up. The British won the toss and shot first, but the rolley holers were soon in control. With Russell leading off, Jack shooting second, and Travis at cleanup, they won by a score of 25 to 6—and it went on like that for most of the morning. The rolley holers tended to win so quickly that they had to rotate their lineup, to give everyone a chance to shoot. They beat some Dutchmen next, and then more British teams than Cherry can really recall, and then they found themselves in the quarterfinals.

There was just one catch—or maybe two. The rolley holers' opponents were Americans as well. And they, not the rolley holers, were the tournament favorites.

In the months preceding the tournament, Fulcher had called a marble manufacturer called Marble King, hoping to get a sponsorship. Rather than pay for the rolley holers, however, Marble King had decided to field its own team, composed of former national ringer champions. Like rolley hole, ringer had made a comeback of late, though on a much larger scale. To become a national champion, you now had to work your way up through regional tournaments, then fight off seventy-five to one hundred other players at the finals in Wildwood, New

Jersey. Moreover ringer was a close cousin to British marbles: it was played on a ten-foot concrete circle—though not covered by sand—and the rules were similar. While the rolley holers were being given a send-off party at Hevi-Duty, the Marble Kings' departure was covered by CBS.

To the spectators at Tinsley Green that day, no two teams seemed more dissimilar, more foreign to each other, than those from America. Where the rolley holers were laconic, the Marble Kings were hyperactive; where the rolley holers' faces barely twitched, no matter how spectacular their shots, the Marble Kings came on like frat boys during homecoming week, pumping their fists and whooping like Comanches. For all their differences, however, the two teams were evenly matched. In the days before the tournament, they had played two exhibition matches. In the first the Marble Kings had won handily; in the second the rolley holers returned the favor.

The deciding match began poorly for the rolley holers. Russell shot first, but though he scattered the marbles nicely around the ring, he failed to knock one off. The other team's shooter, a UPS worker from Cumberland, Maryland, quickly took advantage of the opening, knocking out ten, then eleven, then twelve marbles in a row. If Jack Tinsley missed his next shot, or knocked out only a few, the other team could clinch a victory.

As good a shot as he was, Jack had never won at Standing Stone, and something about his wild beard and occasionally wilder shooting kept the others from taking him entirely seriously. True, his last name seemed an uncommonly good omen, but Jack swore he had no kin at Tinsley Green. All of which made what happened next something of a shock. Stepping up to the concrete circle, dipping his hand into the panty hose between shots, shifting around the circle as calmly as a clock hand, Jack proceeded to shoot out twenty-five marbles in a row, closing out the game.

After that, even the final seemed anticlimactic. The French, having beaten another British team easily, came in strutting like gamecocks. Theirs was the world's most devoted, best-organized marble tradition, with five separate divisions and thousands of registered players. Like the British, the French were used to playing on sand—though their game featured only fifteen marbles, clustered in a triangle—and they had played at Tinsley Green before.

The rolley holers never gave them a chance. Though Russell and Jack both missed this time, Bobby Dyer came through with a streak of his own, and the rolley holers won 25 to 1. "The French, they had tears in their eyes," Fulcher says. "They were ashamed that they had let down their country." When it was all over, and the rolley holers had won a separate round-robin tournament as well—beating the Marble Kings and the French again, as well as a team of British all-stars—they were 11 and 0.

That evening, at a ceremony on the green, Sam McCarthy presented the rolley holers with medallions and a silver cup that had never left England. "They displayed it in the lounge at the Hevi-Duty factory for a while," Fulcher says, "right below the Marble Wall of Fame. But then the British came and took it back."

—

News of the Frenchmen's and Englishmen's losses incited no riots in Lyons, no impromptu scrums in Liverpool. British marble hooligans, such as they were, stayed home and watched the telly. But to people on the upper Cumberland, the World Marble Championship meant more than a dozen World Cups. Elsewhere people have grown used to news that means everything and nothing at the same time—the O.J. Simpson trial, the Monica Lewinsky hearings, the *Seinfeld* finale. But in small-town Kentucky or Tennessee a single story can rattle a community for years. Around there, when you drive down a country road you don't see billboards of Tiger Woods. You see large wooden signs, twenty years old but still freshly painted. "Welcome to ———, Tennessee," they say, "Home of the 1977 Class AAA Women's Volleyball State Champions."

On the Saturday afternoon when Jack Tinsley and the others drove back into Tennessee, a police escort was at the Clay County line to greet them. When the caravan arrived in the town of Celina, sirens blaring and blue lights flashing, there was a platform, balloons, and a small brass band waiting. There were speeches and jokes and, later that summer, a parade at the Watermelon Festival. THUMBS UP, Y'ALL! the headline read on the front page of the Louisville *Courier-Journal*. "Good Ol' Boys Simply Marbleous, Whip World."

Then, for an improbable moment, the rolley holers became media darlings after all, each story inspiring another. Tipped off by the Tennessee papers, ESPN did two segments on the game, one of which featured Fulcher's patented play-by-play ("If he misses this shot, they'll be on him like a pack of wild dogs"). Next *Sports Illustrated* ran a story called "Rolley-Hole Heaven," with a picture of a player caked in dust, bent over so far that his pants were falling off. That picture, in turn, caught the eye of the late cartoonist Charles Schulz, who turned his character Rerun into a rolley hole fanatic. "I'm going to enter the 'Rolley Hole' Championship in Standing Stone State Park in Tennessee," he told Snoopy in one strip. "Wherever that is."

Fulcher did his best to take advantage of the publicity; he even proposed including rolley hole in the folklife festival at the Atlanta Olympic Games. But the rolley holers never did get used to the limelight. It wasn't that they were immune to celebrity—the upper Cumberland has its share of satellite dishes—but they were too humble to brag, too proud to play the clowns, the Hillbilly Globetrotters. And so, often as not, if a city reporter came by, they'd nod politely and feed him lie after lie. When the paper came out the next day, with a picture of a local lush identified as a rolley holer, they'd just grin and pass it around.

—

By the time I met Fulcher, Standing Stone had become something of a Mecca for marble players. Every year some new delegation of foreign players arrived at the tournament to demonstrate their games and gawk at the local shooters. They came from India, Ireland, Mexico, Guatemala, Liberia, and, of course, France and England. And while they came, the local kids—those who used to play for hatfuls of change—were busy leaving, burnishing the rolley hole legend elsewhere. Led by Travis Cherry, they flew to Wildwood, New Jersey, and won four national marbles championships in four years, with Nathan Thompson entering the Marbles Hall of Fame. "That first year we showed up," Cherry says, "they didn't know what hit 'em."

Now back at Standing Stone, through the long afternoon and into the evening, rolley holers shuffled and slouched across the yard that Fulcher built. Years of multicultural marble exhibits and product tie-ins, national championships and marble halls of fame, hadn't changed the roster much since Fulcher stumbled on his first game in the woods. There was Russell Collins, with his slicked-back silver hair and predatory moves, and Ralph Roberts making cracks just under his breath. Here came the perennial parade of brothers: the Rhotens, the Tinsleys, the Bowmans. And there was Nathan Thompson, the Mozart of marbles, all grown up but still as shy and pudgy as ever. Though he'd set the ringer world to sword and flame, he'd never won at Standing Stone—and today was no exception. In the first round his team was set to make the last hole when Jack Tinsley and his brother, Wink, came from behind to knock them out.

If the players were the same, though, nothing else really was. The yard lay under a sleek new roof now, to keep out the hickory nuts and rain; Bud Garrett's rolley hole blues had given way to an earnest announcer; and the game itself had taken on a bit of their gloss, their stiffness. In the old days the size of a marble yard, the distance between holes—even the name of the game—was a matter of imperfect recall, and the rules could be fudged to suit your fancy. If a marble rolled close to a hole, a player might reach over and drop it in, implying it was a sure shot. "Players used to joke that So-and-so had a pretty good reach on 'im," Fulcher says. But once real money was at stake in the tournaments, the old jokes weren't as funny anymore.

To keep the peace, Fulcher had had no choice but to establish the rule of law, like some backwoods King Arthur. He had sent out ballots and made phone calls, printed newsletters and designed a scoreboard ("My first try looked like a plan for building a spaceship"), gradually chiseling rules from rough understandings. The fever, you might say, had burned a new clarity into the game—to be dropped in a hole, for instance, a marble now always had to come within a hand's span of it—but Fulcher knew such clarity came at a cost. Back at Russell Collins's yard the repartee had been nearly as good as the shots. But at Standing Stone the atmosphere was as hushed and expectant as at an Orthodox service.

Sometime well past midnight, Doyle Rhoten and Russell won their fourth tournament, beating out Ralph Roberts and Doyle's older brother, Wayne—a perfect repeat of the first Standing Stone final. By then the bluegrass band in the pavilion nearby had packed up its banjos and the last of the marble vendors had cleared out, leaving only the clicking of flint and the whispering of spectators in the stands. As the night fog moved in and the temperature dropped, the players moved more deliberately, their choreography seemingly preordained. Though the crowd let out a whoop when Wayne shot for the match and missed, the sound had a strange, strangled quality after so many hours of silence. After Fulcher handed out the checks, and the spectators groaned to their feet, the yard emptied out in a matter of minutes. As if it had never held anything but ghosts.

—

Southern summers can idle past so slow and languid, they seem barely to move at all. But the planet grinds back into gear eventually, turning the trees from green to gold to parchment brown. Along the long, looping country roads, you can feel the atmosphere tensing with responsibility, the air insistent with ripening tobacco and fresh resin from the lumber-yards. The world of a marble yard, no matter how challenging or replete with variation, begins to feel confining, repetitious. You get tired of the old wise-cracks and the flushed faces that make them, and even the best games begin to feel unsatisfying.

When I came back to the upper Cumberland in mid-November, rolley hole seemed the furthest thing from people's minds. Fulcher had agreed to take me on a tour of famous rolley hole landmarks—the Marbles Super Dome, the Hevi-Duty plant, the Napa auto parts store where the kids used to practice ringer—but his heart wasn't really in it. Most of the marble yards were deserted now, and everyone agreed that the fever had finally broken. "You came at the wrong time for rolley hole, son," an eighty-year-old player named Preacher Denton told me when we stopped by his house.

Rolley hole had always been an excuse to bring people together, to make peace among factions. But now jealousies were beginning to smolder among teammates—many of them siblings or neighbors. "I've seen old men a-playin' rolley hole and they was havin' the biggest time there ever was, and the biggest fun there ever was," Denton said. "But they get to playin' it too much for blood. And it ain't a sport when you get it that far." Back in the 1920s, when emotions ran that high, a player in Moss, Tennessee, stabbed another to death after a game. In the 1950s it was a player with a tire iron bludgeoning another from behind as he crouched to shoot.

Sitting in a Dairy Queen long after dark, nursing his Dr Pepper, Fulcher wondered if the cycle was repeating itself. Late at night, he said, driving the back roads of rural Tennessee, he would tune his radio to militia stations and listen in on conspiracy theories and government demonologies, talk of black helicopters and secret troop movements. Beneath the dull surface of these country towns, there ran a glimmering vein of paranoia, one forged by isolation and a long history of exploitation. Most of the time you could tamp it down with jokes and goodwill. But a game like rolley hole, in its strange way, was a powder keg. The tournaments and TV interviews, tightening rules and trip to England—all of them had blown the old grudges back to the surface. Cross-border rivalries were flaring between teams from Kentucky and Tennessee, and Fulcher had been accused of favoring players from his home state. "I had this sweet, ninety-year-old woman really get mad at me on the phone one night," he said. "And some of these things, people never get over them their whole lives."

Fulcher lifted his wire-frame glasses and rubbed his eyes for a long moment. But when he was done the weariness was still there—the antic gleam dulled by memories of countless negotiations and small misunderstandings, of faux pas and feuding families and self-doubts always hovering in the shadows. Had his rules sapped the game's spirit? Had the tournaments primed it for another implosion? Only a year before, Fulcher had cooked up an international marbles festival at Standing Stone. He'd brought in local Mexican laborers to demonstrate their games and printed a newsletter with profiles of all the players; he'd set up a round-robin championship and charmed Marble King into donating one ton of marbles for kids' contests. But though he'd filled Standing Stone to capacity, and though he'd nearly short-circuited his marriage with the effort—"His old lady was about fried," Cogswell told me—the crowds hadn't come back this year. In the sere November light it was hard to imagine they'd ever been there at all.

In truth, Fulcher's weariness went beyond the discontents of rolley hole. If folklorists were flush with optimism in the sixties and seventies, embracing banjo pickers and country dances as if they were penniless orphans, by the early nineties they were having second thoughts, eyeing folk revival as suspiciously as welfare. Folk revivals were never more than romantic fictions, some said. Like the refrains of the old ballads themselves, they rolled around every other generation or so, echoing with melancholy and tales of loss, but the authenticity they sought was a chimera, constantly receding. Twenty years before Fulcher drove into the hills, Alan Lomax was recording chain gangs and field hollers in Mississippi, resurrecting the country blues; twenty years before that, eastern record scouts were dressing up the Carter family as hillbilly minstrels, selling the "real America" to jaded urbanites; twenty years before that, Cecil Sharpe was collecting Elizabethan ballads in the Kentucky coal country, declaring that "posterity will need the primitive songs" to keep "music and dance real, sincere, and pure." But those "primitive songs" were themselves facsimiles, their purity corrupted long ago.

Even if you can find a tradition with deep, undamaged roots, more and more critics were saying, there's no use trying to "save" it. You'll only corrupt what was once most true—turning it into a shadow of itself at best, a travesty at worst. Better to let a tradition run its course—to die of natural causes or disappear into the thicket of popular culture—than to jolt it alive for one last turn around the fairground.

Like most of the musicians he'd known, Fulcher had spent his youth recklessly free-associating, spinning off ideas without a care for where they landed. But his son, Russell, had been born the year before, and the experience had left him "goofy crazy" about fatherhood and hungry for some kind of permanence. Lately, Fulcher had quit going to folklore meetings altogether and was focusing on conservation work instead. "I guess I felt that the people I cared about personally were dying off," he said. "And if you can't haul that flesh-and-blood person in front of other people, all that's left, in the vinyl of that record, is just a shadow. It approaches being meaningless. I mean, when some eighteen-year-old city kid plays 'Whoa, Mule, Whoa,' what does that mean to him? Not the same as to Grandpa, who had to hold on to that mule. Not the same as to that old red-faced man standing up there laughing and singing it, looking around for that glint of recognition in his audience."

He paused, as if startled by his own words. "I love the arts," he said. "But I've kind of lost faith in their ability to sweep broadly through the world. I know that they can bloom, the way zydeco did a while back. But lately here, I've been thinking if I'm going to bust and sweat to do something for the world, I ought to do it for making it a greener place. Somehow, if you can set aside a gorgeous piece of the world, it seems like that's going to have more longevity."

Rolley hole had been the great exception, his last stab at revival. And for a time, at least, it had worked: Fulcher hadn't strong-armed the players into picking up the game again. He hadn't dressed them up in traditional costumes or taken them on educational tours of the local schools. He'd just built a marble yard and offered some prize money, and the players had done the rest. "Rolley hole just had a little dust on it," he liked to say, "and we just kind of knocked it off." But now, with attendance down and a vague discontent in the air, old-timers switching over to Tennessee Square and kids switching to ringer, Fulcher had to wonder. Was rolley hole just taking a breather, or had it become a kind of Frankenstein after all? Was its heart still pumping, or was it lumbering along on his electricity alone?

Later that night, as I climbed out of Fulcher's truck to say good-bye, he hesitated for just a moment before pulling the door shut. "The future of rolley hole is as hard to predict as the weather," he said, glancing down the road, "and only a fool would try to do either one."

—

On a dim, overcast afternoon, with winter hovering in the wings, I drove out to the Super Dome one last time, not expecting to find anyone home. Back in 1989, when the fever was burning strong, rolley holers were so hot to play year-round that they built an indoor marble yard here: a low-slung, swaybacked shed on the outskirts of Tompkinsville, Kentucky, by the Monroe County fairgrounds. In its heyday the Super Dome had sixty-four members and there were two marble yards under the roof, running side by side till past midnight. But today the fairgrounds were empty and sodden, and the town seemed to brood behind its shutters. Jostling down the gravel drive, I was already looking for a turnaround ahead when I noticed a thin, twisting cloud above the chimney: a smoke signal of the most basic kind.

Inside, Earl Coulter was cramming a tree stump into the potbellied stove, the sparks showering around his bare ankles and tennis shoes. "It's about as dead as it seems," he said, plopping back into his seat with a grunt. He looked around, distracted, at the corrugated metal walls and broken windows, the secondhand sofas and crippled chairs, the handmade sign that said "Monroe County Marble Club, 1998 membership." There were nine names on it—Earl's at the top—scrawled in black Magic Marker. "Only half of them have paid," he said, chewing his lower lip. "But we've had them Mormon boys come down here lately. They couldn't hardly shoot a marble at first, but now they've gotten pretty good." He stopped, his squinty, stubbled features darkening suddenly. "'Course, it's a different thing, ridin' them bicycles over here in the winter."

Earl lived just inside city limits, in a dilapidated trailer house, with a Native American woman who was something of a mystery to the other players. He had no phone, no mailbox, no real job. To scrape a living together, he drove around town in his dinged-up orange truck, picking up odd jobs and janitorial work, sorting through vacuum-cleaner dust for coins ("I've already got half a quart jar," he said, "and it won't be long before it's full. People just throw money away"). Whenever I saw him he seemed to be wearing the same outfit: grimy jeans and a camouflaged duck-hunting cap, a red flannel vest so wash-worn it looked pink, and a big button that said "Sports Illustrated All-Star"—"Them reporters give it to me when they was down here," he said. "Put me on TV down in Nashville, too." On his hip he wore a bright red radio that squawked reports to volunteer firemen, but he ignored it whenever he was at the Super Dome.

To the other players, Earl was an entertainment, the court fool. They called him the King of Marbles in the same vein that they called this the Super Dome. But Earl lived for rolley hole. Back at his trailer he'd been writing a book about the game in longhand, on a thick Indian Head writing tablet. He couldn't seem to get it finished, he said, couldn't find the time to take it over to the copy shop. But he could tell the tale of Tinsley Green as if reciting epic poetry, and he kept an oral history of rolley hole players in his head at all times.

"I don't mix myself in other folks' business 'cause I got enough of my own to take care of," he said, starting off with his usual disclaimer. "But if you ask me, there's something fishy about a man who comes from California, don't know anybody, and gets a job in the poorest county in Kentucky. Now, some folks said he was with the FBI." He paused, letting the words hang in the air. "I don't know about that. All I know is he got to playin' pretty good and then he got bad, so that he could hardly hit the broad side of a barn. He lost at Hevi-Duty and he lost at Standing Stone, and then it seemed like he didn't care no more. He was hitting the bottle too hard, if you ask me, and so on, so forth, on down the line."

Earl never did mention the man's name, but I'd heard the same lament half a dozen times before— rolley holers lost to drink, to drugs, to softball, or to golf, the causes all equal, somehow, as long as they led to this effect: the Super Dome empty and Earl tending the fire alone. "I come out here three or four nights a week," he said. "Some nights there ain't hardly enough people to get a game." But then, as if on cue, a rattle of steel sounded through the side door, and tires crunched to a halt on the gravel outside. There were blunt voices and slamming doors, and suddenly the room seemed to be full of people—three more of them, to be exact. They must have known that Earl would be there to make a fourth.

Within moments they were out on the yard, rolling their marbles toward the hole to see who would go first, settling into their old rhythm as if picking up a conversation.

"Was that pretty?"

"No, *that's* pretty."

"That's the prettiest shot I ever did see."

Earl was teamed with Laurence Scott, a well-groomed older gentleman in starched denim shirt and pants—the kind of man you expect to see on a putting green wearing Munsingwear—while the opposing team was led by Fred Tooley, a hulking, pop-eyed galoot with a crimson face, a proudly distended belly, and surprisingly delicate hands. Though a few of their shots were still spectacular, they'd misfire often as not, and the rules were as loose as the talk. For easy approach shots they'd toss their marbles under-hand, or even kick them, and Laurence was so stiff with arthritis he'd drop his marble into the hole whenever it came close.

No one seemed to mind. "It's your hole, I've got a ride," Tooley's partner, Jim Biggerstaff, said. He meant he had a clear shot on Earl's marble and from there to the hole.

"If you can ride that, I'll kiss you."

"Well, I might just have to miss it, then."

Tooley crouched down to shoot, his butt crack rising above his jeans. When he was done he leaped up and down as if stung by a hornet, chewing his fingers like a little girl and letting off a high-pitched squeal. Instead of knocking out Earl's marble, as he intended, he'd merely nicked it in passing, leaving Earl's marble in place and his own out of position. "You pulled his hair," Biggerstaff said, using the same term that the Cherokee use.

And so the marbles rolled and the quips clipped by, and soon enough they were "all for outs," maneuvering around the final hole like predators and prey around an oasis. Earl wanted to sink his marble and go out, but if he did it too soon, his opponents would gang up on his partner. His first task, therefore, was to knock Tooley and Biggerstaff's marbles out of range.

Shuffling his hands in the dust, Earl squinted with one eye and tugged on his duckbill hat, lining up his shot.

"You got 'im, Earl?"

"I'm not promising anything."

"Have you got 'im?"

"I'll try."

"Make it, Earl! Make it now!"

Earl knuckled down for the kill, his pale marble smooth and pure against his chapped and weathered hands, his bedeviled eyes suddenly clear, his hands steadier than they ever were stoking the fire or sifting for change. Then his marble shot out, tracing a perfect arc above the yard, flying toward the deadlock with all the goodwill and stubborn optimism in the world. And landed plumb in the hole.

"Oh, Earl . . ."

"You're out, Earl."

Earl tried meekly to play dumb—"I laid it in the hole?"—but he knew the game, for all intents and purposes, was lost.

266 ○§ *Burkhard Bilger*

"Yes, you did, Earl, you laid it in the hole."

"You was too excited about runnin' over him, I guess."

"But you played an awful good game."

Earl had had enough, and the others were there only for a game or two. As they shuffled out the door, still chuckling about Earl's last shot, Tooley turned to me and said, "Southern pastimes? Why don't you write one about Earl chasin' two fat women around?"

But Earl was right behind him. "If someone ever wrote a book about my personal life, it'd blow their minds."

Then they were gone, and the Super Dome was as empty as Standing Stone had been, though the embers were still burning in the stove. And I thought about what Fulcher had told me the day before, when we'd walked out onto the yards at the Hevi-Duty plant and found them overgrown with weeds. "Doesn't look like they've been playing much lately," I joked, trying to make light of his discouragement. But he turned and frowned. "No, no, these courts were used just a few weeks ago." He pulled up a handful of weeds and showed me their bulbous, muddy roots. "These are winter annuals. See, their seeds are just below the ground, waiting to germinate at the end of the fall."

And so it may be with rolley hole. A good game is a tough thing, hard to kill. It can float through the history of a place like dandelion seed—wispy, wind-blown, barely alive. It can disappear for generations, waiting for some secret change in the atmosphere, some long drink of rain. And then one bright spring morning along a forgotten stretch of road, its blossoms will suddenly blanket the fields, sunstruck and perfect, an apotheosis of weeds. As if some patient gardener has been planning this all along.

Acknowledgments

Traveling south and southwest these past few years has been a tremendous pleasure, but not without its uneasy moments. Depending on my subject, I've felt like an insider or an anthropologist, a devotee or a double agent, and some of my sources must have shared my doubts. As a man in Atlanta told me one afternoon, when I asked him where I could eat some boiled pig's ears: "What you doin' here, white boy?"

Still, it would be hard to imagine kinder hosts than the people in these stories. They've put me up for days at a time, let me sleep on their couches or floors, and endured endless interviews and follow-up calls. Their generosity has often been in inverse proportion to their risk in talking to me. Although I can't properly thank some of them here, I hope they will read their names between the lines of these acknowledgments. As for the rest, I'll mention only those, among hundreds of helpful sources, to whom I owe the greatest debt.

James Demoruelle initiated me into the world of cockfighting when chances were I meant to condemn it. Keith Sutton taught me the history of noodling and showed me how it's done, and Lee McFarlin sent me home with fish enough for five families. Steve Rector and Sondra Beck took me into their families, though they had only a phone call to go on, and took me hunting, though I must have scared off half their game. Tim Patridge stuffed me with more fine meals than I thought I could hold, and the men of the Moonshine Task Force—Jimmy Beheler, J. E. Calhoun, Gerald Joyce, Bev Whitmer, and Randall Toney—told me more good stories than one chapter can contain. May their Hollywood dreams come true.

I'm obliged to Jon Donlon and Shelly Drummond for giving me short courses in the politics of culture, to Ken Holyoak for leading me on some wonderful hog, frog, and wild-goose chases, and to chef David Berry for taking my bag of bloody game and turning it into one of the best meals I've ever eaten. Bob Fulcher and Jeff Jackson were not only incomparable hosts, they put much of what I learned elsewhere in context, showing me the lay of the territory and its distant sweep, as only real insider-anthropologists can.

This book could not have been written without some equally important help back home. Elizabeth

Ziemska helped inspire the project, and my agent, Elyse Cheney, brought it to completion with aplomb. My editor, Gillian Blake, offered invaluable advice as I wrote the manuscript, and my fact checker, Keely Savoie, saved me from more than one embarrassment. When I needed a leave of absence from *The Sciences*, where I worked during most of the book's composition, editor Peter Brown granted it with his usual graciousness. When I needed quiet places (with great food) to hole up and write, I found them with my parents, Hans and Edeltraut Bilger; with my wife's parents, Ted and Gerada Nelson; with my brother and sister-in-law, Dan Nelson and Audrey Luna; and with my friend Todd Wiener. When I needed good advice, or just a reminder that there is life after squirrel brains, I got them from my brother Martin, my sisters, Eva, Monika, and Andrea, and my brother and sister-in-law, George Black and Anne Nelson. Most of all, my wife, Jennifer Nelson, and my children, Hans and Ruby, deserve my gratitude. They put up with all my working weekends and research trips, night sweats, vacant stares, and passages read aloud. I won't say they never grumbled, but they did so in the nicest possible way, and their love and support saw me through.

Finally, I'd like to acknowledge—however uselessly—those who truly risked their lives—however inadvertently—to make many of these stories possible: the catfish and fighting cocks, bullfrogs, raccoons, and squirrels that were often fleeing the people I was chasing. Although this is largely a chronicle of happy hunting, that phrase seems to grow more contested, more contradictory, every year. By stabbing at our conscience, animals illuminate our changing values; by dying out or growing scarce, they make vivid our shrinking wilderness; by outwitting our best-laid plans for them, they demonstrate the limits to our dominion.

Long may they run.

Permissions